THE BECKET CONTROVERSY

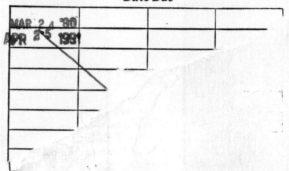

MAJOR ISSUES IN HISTORY

Editor
C. WARREN HOLLISTER,
University of California, Santa Barbara

THE BECKET
CONTROVERSY

EDITED BY

Thomas M. Jones

John Wiley and Sons, Inc.

New York London Sydney Toronto

DA
209
T4
J6
1970

Library of Congress Catalogue Card Number: 78-110171 7.9.74

Cloth: SBN 471 44755 2
Paper: SBN 471 44756 0

Printed in the United States of America

10 9 8 7 6 5 4 3 2 1

SERIES PREFACE

The reading program in a history survey course traditionally has consisted of a large two-volume textbook and, perhaps, a book of readings. This simple reading program requires few decisions and little imagination on the instructor's part, and tends to encourage in the student the virtue of careful memorization. Such programs are by no means things of the past, but they certainly do not represent the wave of the future.

The reading program in survey courses at many colleges and universities today is far more complex. At the risk of over-simplification, and allowing for many exceptions and overlaps, it can be divided into four categories: (1) textbook, (2) original source readings, (3) specialized historical essays and interpretive studies, and (4) historical problems.

After obtaining an overview of the course subject matter (textbook), sampling the original sources, and being exposed to selective examples of excellent modern historical writing (historical essays), the student can turn to the crucial task of weighing various possible interpretations of major historical issues. It is at this point that memory gives way to creative critical thought. The "problems approach," in other words, is the intellectual climax of a thoughtfully conceived reading program and is, indeed, the most characteristic of all approaches to historical pedagogy among the newer generation of college and university teachers.

The historical problems books currently available are many and varied. Why add to this information explosion? Because the Wiley Major Issues Series constitutes an endeavor to produce something new that will respond to pedagogical needs thus far unmet. First, it is a series of individual volumes—one per problem. Many good teachers would much prefer to select their own historical issues rather than be tied to an inflexible sequence of issues imposed by a publisher and bound together between two covers. Second, the Wiley Major Issues Series is based on the idea of approaching the significant problems of history through a deft interweaving of primary sources and secondary analysis, fused together by the skill of a scholar-editor. It is felt that the essence of a historical issue cannot be satisfactorily probed either by placing a body of undigested source materials into the hands of inexperienced students or by limiting these students to the controversial literature of modern scholars who debate the meaning of sources the student never sees. This series approaches historical problems by exposing students to both the finest historical thinking on the issue and some of the evidence on which this thinking is based. This synthetic approach should prove far more fruitful than either the raw-source approach or the exclusively second-hand approach, for it combines the advantages— and avoids the serious disadvantages—of both.

Finally, the editors of the individual volumes in the Major Issues Series have been chosen from among the ablest scholars in their fields. Rather than faceless referees, they are historians who know their issues from the inside and, in most instances, have themselves contributed significantly to the relevant scholarly literature. It has been the editorial policy of this series to permit the editor-scholars of the individual volumes the widest possible latitude both in formulating their topics and in organizing their materials. Their scholarly competence has been unquestioningly respected; they have been encouraged to approach the problems as they see fit. The titles and themes of the series volumes have been suggested in nearly every case by the scholar-editors themselves. The criteria have been (1) that the issue be of relevance to undergraduate lecture courses in history, and (2) that it be an issue which the scholar-editor knows thoroughly and in which he has done creative work. And, in general, the second criterion has been given precedence over the first. In short, the question "What are the significant historical issues today?" has been answered not by general editors or sales departments but by the scholar-teachers who are responsible for these volumes.

University of California,   C. *Warren Hollister*
Santa Barbara

CONTENTS

THE BECKET CONTROVERSY

INTRODUCTION

The murder of Archbishop Thomas Becket in 1170 produced an immediate sense of shock that can be recognized by a generation similarly stunned by President Kennedy's assassination. A better parallel would be the death of Dr. Martin Luther King because he, like Becket, was the victim of a society polarized by two sets of opposing forces.

Becket's murder climaxed a seven-year power struggle. Sounds and echoes of the struggle have fascinated generations of historians as well as playwrights, novelists, and poets ever since. To the classic issues that divided church and state were added elements of personal drama involving two strong-willed antagonists who had once been close personal friends and colleagues.

When Henry II became king of England in 1154, one of his first acts was to appoint men whose loyalty, administrative skills, and tireless energy he could depend upon. One such man was Thomas Becket. A clerk and then an archdeacon of Canterbury, Becket was elevated to the office of chancellor within the first year of the new reign. In this capacity he served as Henry's chief envoy, led at least one military expedition, and assisted in creating order out of the confusion that had marked the twenty years of disputed rule that preceded Henry's reign.

Although Henry was fourteen years younger than Becket, the two men became constant social companions. They hunted together, ate and drank together, and shared adventurous excitement at a frenetic pace. Born to neither nobility nor wealth, Becket quickly learned the social patterns of both. While he was chancellor, his lavish clothing and richly decorated table impressed contemporary chroniclers, whose descriptions suggest the ostentation of the nouveaux riches.

In April 1161, Theobald, archbishop of Canterbury, died. To succeed him, Henry wanted to appoint an ally who would share the royal vision of a strong central monarchy. With an archbishop sympathetic to royal interests, Henry could strengthen the king's courts at the expense of the increasingly independent church courts, and in other ways he could build a more powerful state dominated by the crown, unthreatened by the parallel leadership of the episcopacy. The ally Henry chose was his chancellor, Thomas Becket. The cathedral chapter of Canterbury elected Becket as the new archbishop in spite of some dissent. The strongest opposition was expressed by Gilbert Foliot, then bishop of Hereford but later bishop of London, and for the next few years Becket's unrelenting opponent.

Once installed as archbishop, Becket made it clear that he was nobody's pawn. He resigned as the king's chancellor, thus demonstrating his full commitment to his new status and symbolically rejecting his old. The resignation had particular force because it contradicted the king's wishes. Thereafter a series of incidents pitted the archbishop's position against the king's, culminating at the moment when Becket fell as a martyr on the floor of Canterbury cathedral.

Becket insisted that certain lands within his diocese be taken from their lay occupants and restored to church control. This revived an old dispute between rival claimants that had already caused an outcry against ecclesiastical land-grabbing. The archbishop's claim to all clerical patronage within his diocese created a further issue. Finally, and most seriously, arose the tangled question of supremacy in courts that handled clerical as well as lay interests. Exemption of clergy from punishment fitting their crimes particularly angered the king and his legal advisors, because Henry II had determined to provide a brand of justice that was both profitable and equitable.

Inevitably the clash over issues merged into a clash of personalities. Henry was a man who did not restrain his anger, either in public or in private. Chroniclers were impressed by frightening epithets like "By the eyes of God!" or "by God's teeth!" roaring out of the king's throat. By the time of the Council of Woodstock in 1163, Henry's hostility toward Thomas was open and widely confirmed; the archbishop was the new object of the Angevin rage. On his part, Becket had developed the unyielding stubbornness that marked the whole controversy.

Early the next year the king summoned the famous council at Clarendon, where he tried to get written agreement from the bishops listing the precise customs of the land that were to be followed in church-state disputes. Generalized promises to abide by vaguely worded customs Archbishop Thomas accepted; specific definitions of what the customs were he rejected. The Constitutions of Clarendon (see below) opened a glaring breach between the realm of Caesar and the realm of God in twelfth century England. Although he refused to affix his seal, Becket, under strong pressure, seems to have acknowledged the constitutions by his acceptance of a copy, but almost immediately after the council and increasingly as time passed he expressed his disapproval of them.

In October of the same year the antagonists faced each other again at Northampton. Barely avoiding defeat, Becket survived a real or feigned illness, finally appeared in a dramatic confrontation with the king, and then chose the path of escape. Those few days at Northampton, marking an emotional climax to the controversy, are described below in an article by Dom David Knowles.

From Northampton, Becket crossed the channel to France, where he stayed in exile for six years. Returning to Canterbury late in the year 1170, he renewed sentences of excommunication against his opponents and delivered a Christmas message that was defiant and provocative. The king responded with one of his furious bursts of anger, raging against his lay vassals for permitting anyone thus to insult their sovereign. Four knights who thought they properly understood Henry's mood hurried across the channel to Kent and made their way to Becket's presence. Contemporary biographers have described in detail the next few hours. Meeting his assailants in the sacrosanct cathedral, Becket defied them to act. Act they did, leaving him dead beside the altar.

As with any historical crisis, the issues of the controversy are many-sided. There is the ageless question of power between the king, secular head of his state, and the primate of the church, spiritual guardian of the people. The nature of this power struggle was by no means simple. It was not a question of being for or against the church, nor was it a question of being for or against the kind of secular justice that Henry's reign represented. The issues of Becket's time had grown in complexity since Lanfranc and Anselm were archbishops, even though both those men also had disputes with their respective monarchs. Institutional development was enormous in late twelfth century England, and neither faction could behave as if patterns were static. The co-existence permitted by the traditional theory of two swords, one civil and one religious, was inappropriate for a king who intended to carry the only sword.

The issue of jurisdiction in the courts was a central problem. Henry, who knew that efficient, firm, decisive justice paid off both financially and administratively, was determined to provide a uniform law common to all the land. In the looseness of the church courts he saw too easy an escape from his conception of justice. Through the Constitutions of Clarendon, the king's legal talent found ways of blocking these escape routes. The archbishop and his followers were unwilling to make serious concessions because they feared that compromise would lead to the end of an independent church.

From William I to Henry VIII, monarchs viewed appeals from England to the pope as threats to their full sovereignty. Two centuries after Becket's death, when the Statute of Praemunire finally made such appeals illegal, England was well on the road toward separation from the Roman church. Henry II wanted the bishops to concur in his judgment that appeals to Rome, overstepping the king, were contrary to established custom and therefore invalid. Precedents for his position did exist, but Becket refused to be the one to affirm the church's acceptance of the point. Not content with vagueness, Henry wanted a clear, unequivocal statement that appeals would stop. The two forces clashed steadily and mightily over this point.

"Customs of the land" could be interpreted in different ways. Becket claimed the right to nominate any clerks within his diocese; the lord of Eynesford, supported by King Henry, interpreted "customs of the land" to give him the right as baron to appoint a clerk within his fief. The king naturally backed his tenant against the conflicting claim of the archbishop. Further, Becket tried to assert his control over the powerful castle at Rochester, and on the same principle demanded custody over various other strategic properties.

Both sides resorted increasingly to rhetoric, and attempts to seek logic and rationality were lost in the emotional turmoil of the conflict. When settlement seemed close, one or the other antagonist refused the small remaining concession. Becket's insistence on the qualifying phrase "saving our order", or Henry's refusal at a critical juncture to grant the "kiss of peace", broke off negotiations that had very nearly healed the breach. The intricacy of the diplomatic as well as the domestic situation compounded the trouble and made it difficult to find any simplistic solution.

During the 1160's the church hierarchy was itself far from solidified in a single position. Thus it would be a serious error to think of a united body of prelates standing together against a common enemy. From the papacy on through local parishes various issues split the clergy. In England two archbishops, one based in the north at York and the other at Canterbury, inherited jealously guarded prerogatives that sometimes overlapped and sometimes encouraged inroads into the other's authority. Thomas Becket's counterpart at York was Roger of Pont-l'Évêque, who from the beginning showed personal as well as professional animosity toward Becket.

At stake was Canterbury's authority as the first metropolitan see, holding primacy over the diocese of York; conversely the archbishop of York was determined to show his independence from the archbishop of Canterbury. A series of episodes tested the relative powers of each. The crucial incident in the series took place early in 1170 when Roger undertook to preside over the coronation of Henry II's son, also named Henry. Passion for administrative orderliness, combined with fresh memories of the preceding reign, when the throne had been claimed by two disputing rivals, led Henry II to see that his son was formally crowned and ready to rule before his own death. The archbishop of Canterbury traditionally performed coronations, and still does, but from 1164 to 1170 the incumbent archbishop was in self-imposed exile. Roger of York, who had already bid for supremacy by seeking to be named as papal legate, agreed to crown the young king, and in so doing he tried to topple the precedent that had reserved that function for the primate at Canterbury.

Becket reacted predictably, with a blast of denunciations not

only against the archbishop of York but against all bishops who
had the temerity to attend the crowning. Only a few months
later Becket was killed, so the issue was unresolved in his lifetime.
In the interval before Becket's death, Henry assured Thomas that
he, as archbishop of Canterbury, would be invited to conduct the
ceremony in proper fashion when he returned to England from
his exile. The effect of the martyrdom was such that on this point
as on many others Canterbury triumphed.

Gilbert Foliot, mentioned above as a consistent opponent of
Becket, revived another claim that would have weakened the
archbishop's supremacy. Once established as bishop of London,
Foliot proposed that his see should be designated as an archdio-
cese with himself as archbishop. Had this been granted, London
could easily have become the religious as well as the political
center of southern England, and Canterbury's primacy would
have been seriously threatened if not terminated.

Beyond England the papacy itself was split, as it was many
times between 1100 and 1400. The split affected the Becket affair.
While Pope Alexander III remained steadily loyal to Becket, his
position was never strong enough to allow the full weight of the
church to oppose Henry in the way that Innocent III was later
able to overwhelm King John. Rival claimants to the papacy,
Victor IV and later Paschal III, had the backing of the Holy
Roman Emperor, Frederick I. Henry therefore could keep Alexander from giving forceful support to Becket by the threat of
transfering allegiance to Frederick's pope. Since the church itself
was not united, and since the king could turn to powerful allies,
the political balance remained favorable to Henry.

The king of France, Louis VII, willingly offered a haven to
Becket during his exile, and had Louis been a more effective
adversary he might have weakened Henry's position significantly.
For more than a decade Louis had watched his royal rival gain
territory, prestige, and even a queen at his expense, so it was
natural that he should support the archbishop's cause and provide
him with safe asylum. Thus Becket became a figure in the long
rivalry of the two kingdoms.

East of France lay the Holy Roman Empire, where Frederick I's term as emperor (1152–90) coincided almost exactly with
Henry II's reign (1154–89). Frederick had his own fight with

the church, with Italy as chief battleground. The shifting cur-
rents of twelfth century diplomacy led the emperor to look for
Henry's backing, with the lure of isolating both the French king
and the legitimate pope. Alexander managed not to lose England
to the antipope, but until the threat of defection had passed, he
found it wiser to negotiate and even procrastinate rather than
deepen the antagonisms over Becket.

Even parts of Italy, where the pope, the Norman barons of the
south, Emperor Frederick I, and the newly flourishing towns
of the north all battled for positions of greater power, became an
arena for Henry's diplomacy. At least one writer has suggested
that the king's interest in Sicily, where he arranged a marriage
for one of his daughters, was part of a grand scheme to isolate
Becket from papal support. While evidence for this view is slim,
it suggests how vast the diplomatic horizon had become.

A purely fictional dimension to the quarrel has identified
Becket as a Saxon, thus opposing a native against a Norman a
century after the conquest. James Babington Macauley, for
instance, called Becket "the first Englishman who, since the Conquest, had been terrible to the foreign tyrants."[1] This anachro-
nistic picture of the conflict as a national rivalry has intrigued
a number of writers, including the twentieth century playwright
Jean Anouilh. Becket's Norman ancestry is reasonably well established, but the temptation to romanticize the quarrel in fictitious terms has been irresistible to many writers.

Another tempting digression is to see the archbishop as a champion of popular rights and liberties, a twelfth century Che Gue-
vera waving a cross instead of a red banner. Bishop William
Stubbs, for example, wrote: "But whatever were the cause which
he was maintaining, he had some part of the glory that belongs
to all who vindicate liberty, to all who uphold weakness against
overwhelming strength."[2] T. S. Eliot's verse play "Murder in the
Cathedral" has the chorus represent the poor women of the
countryside, with the archbishop as their champion. Others have
found him to be villainous rather than heroic; it is hard to be
indifferent to the legendary Becket.

---

[1] Macauley, *History of England*, Vol. I, p. 18.
[2] Stubbs, *The Early Plantaganets*, p. 83.

Great historical episodes can acquire histories of their own quite separate from the record of what actually happened. Thus, promptly after Becket's death several contemporaries who had known him wrote biographies that were uniformly laudatory but still of value, because they contain some facts and many opinions that might soon have been forgotten. John of Salisbury, friend and supporter of Thomas, and one of the brilliant scholars of his age, wrote such an account. So did Edward Grim, William Fitz Stephen, Herbert of Bosham, and others. Most chronicles repeated ritualistically the praises of the sainted martyr, but William of Newburgh, who dared to suggest the presence of human and political flaws in Becket's behavior, wrote a history in the late 1100's that is remarkable for its critical objectivity.

Until the separation of the English church from Rome in the sixteenth century, Becket remained a figure of heroic mold, attracting masses of pilgrims to his shrine, including the motley group that Chaucer immortalized. Renaissance humanists began to scorn medieval saints just as they scorned Gothic architecture, and Becket had his share of discreditors throughout the sixteenth and seventeenth centuries. In the eighteenth century, Lord Lyttelton's lengthy biography of Henry was countered by a defense of Becket written by the Reverend Joseph Berington.

Scholars of the nineteenth century began a rigorous examination of the primary sources. Once again loyalties divided, and the issues of the 1160's were fought with the pens of historians from the Victorian era. Writers of the first half of the twentieth century have seemed less eager to take sides in the controversy. Issues other than the right to trial in a bishop's court have so overwhelmed the generation of the atom bomb that the occasional revival of the quarrel has usually involved only legend and fancy.

Just as each generation writes its own history, so each generation develops its own controversies. Every century has managed to read old crises in the language of its own problems. Understanding this, the student must seek to recover the remains of perennial truth in a controversy that is eight hundred years old.

PART ONE

Twelfth Century Materials

TWELFTH CENTURY MATERIALS

1   *The Constitutions of Clarendon*

Central to the whole controversy was the document collectively labelled "the Constitutions of Clarendon." The term "constitutions" refers here simply to a set of principles each separately identified as a summary of an established custom; Clarendon was the place in south-central England where the deliberations took place.

As usual in royal charters, the document commences with a listing of those present who witnessed it, and we find here the names of the various bishops who were involved in the affair. According to the opening paragraph, Becket and his colleagues accepted viva voce *the itemized customs, but the archbishop later withdrew his approval and asked papal forgiveness for having momentarily accepted them.*

Many of the points in the constitutions introduced the basic disputes outstanding between crown and church. The issues raised in points 4 and 8 concerned appeals beyond the king to the pope at Rome. The king, determined to be the final voice in judicial disputes in his land, rejected the right of anyone in England to appeal beyond him for a papal hearing. Through points 5, 7, and 10 the king tried to prevent the weapon of excommunication from being used as a countermeasure against his supporters. Points 1, 3, 6, and 9 dealt with thorny matters of judicial procedure, with Henry naturally emphasizing precedents that strengthened the royal courts.

The clerical party, supported by Pope Alexander III, was most concerned about those articles that weakened appeals to the pope or that significantly weakened church courts. Article 3 (discussed in some detail in the selection by Professor Barlow) was basic to the whole dispute. The pope expressed serious reservations about the two articles, 4 and 8, that denied appeals to the papacy; he also wished

SOURCE. "The Constitutions of Clarendon (1164)," *Sources of English Constitutional History*, edited and translated by Carl Stephenson and Frederick George Marcham, pp. 73–76. Copyright 1937, 1965 by Harper & Row, Inc. Reprinted by permission of the publishers.

the church to retain full control over the powerful weapon of excommunication.

On the other hand, there were parts of the constitutions that the pope did not seriously challenge. The clergy had no wish to undermine the feudal practices that required the performance of obligations to a lord, or to undermine the feudal authority of the king. For example, articles 11 and 12 were not in dispute, although there was some question about the king's insistence on conducting episcopal elections in his own chapel.

The real fear that the constitutions aroused among the bishops, including even Becket's opponents, was that the church would be reduced to a secondary status as royal power expanded. In this sense the debate over this document was part of the wider struggle between pope and crown that continued throughout most of the eleventh and twelfth centuries.

In the year 1164 from the Incarnation of the Lord, in the fourth year of the papacy of Alexander [III], and in the twelfth year of Henry II, most illustrious king of the English, there was made, in the presence of the said king, this record and recognition of a certain portion of the customs and liberties and rights of his ancestors—namely, of King Henry his grandfather and of others —which ought to be observed and held in the kingdom. And on account of the dissensions and disputes that had arisen between the clergy and the justices of the lord king and the barons of the realm concerning [such] customs and rights, this recognition was made in the presence of the archbishops, bishops, clergy, earls, barons, and magnates of the realm. Furthermore, Thomas, archbishop of Canterbury, and Roger, archbishop of York, and Gilbert, bishop of London, and Henry, bishop of Winchester, and Nigel, bishop of Ely, and William, bishop of Norwich, and Robert, bishop of Lincoln, and Hilary, bishop of Chichester, and Jocelyn, bishop of Salisbury, and Richard, bishop of Chester, and Bartholomew, bishop of Exeter, and Robert, bishop of Hereford, and David, bishop of St. David's and Roger, [bishop] elect of Worcester, have granted and steadfastly promised, *viva voce* and on their word of truth, that the said customs, recognized by the archbishops, bishops, earls, and barons, and by the nobler and more venerable men of the realm, should be held and observed for the lord king and his heirs in good faith and without evil intent, these being present . . . and many other magnates and nobles of the realm, both clerical and lay.

Now a certain part of the recognized customs and rights of the kingdom are contained in the present writing, of which part these are the chapters:

1. If controversy arises between laymen, between laymen and clergymen, or between clergymen, with regard to advowson and presentation to churches, it shall be treated or concluded in the court of the lord king.

2. Churches of the lord king's fee may not be given in perpetuity without his assent and grant.

3. Clergymen charged and accused of anything shall, on being summoned by a justice of the king, come into his court, to be responsible there for whatever it may seem to the king's court they should there be responsible for; and [to be responsible] in the ecclesiastical court [for what] it may seem they should there be responsible for—so that the king's justice shall send into the court of Holy Church to see on what ground matters are there to be treated. And if the clergyman is convicted, or [if he] confesses, the Church should no longer protect him.

4. Archbishops, bishops, and parsons of the kingdom are not permitted to go out of the kingdom without the licence of the lord king. And should they go out [of it], they shall, if the king so desires, give security that, neither in going nor in remaining nor in returning, will they seek [to bring] evil or damage to the king or to the kingdom.

5. Excommunicated men should not give security for all future time or take an oath, but [should] merely [provide] security and pledge of standing by the judgment of the church in order to obtain absolution.

6. Laymen should not be accused except through known and lawful accusers and witnesses in the presence of the bishop, [yet] so that the archdeacon shall not lose his right or anything that he should thence have. And if the guilty persons are such that no one wishes or dares to accuse them, the sheriff, on being asked by the bishop, shall have twelve lawful men from the neighbour-

hood, or the vill, placed on oath before the bishop to set forth the truth in the matter according to their own knowledge.

7. No one who holds of the king in chief, nor any of his demesne ministers, shall be excommunicated; nor shall the lands of any of them be placed under interdict, unless first the lord king, if he is in the land, or his justiciar, if he is outside the kingdom, agrees that justice shall be done on that person—and in such a way that whatever belongs to the king's court shall be settled there, and whatever belongs to the ecclesiastical court shall be sent thither to be dealt with there.

8. With regard to appeals, should they arise—they should proceed from the archdeacon to the bishop, and from the bishop to the archbishop. And if the archbishop fails to provide justice, recourse should finally be had to the lord king, in order that by his precept the controversy may be brought to an end in the court of the archbishop; so that it should not proceed farther without the assent of the lord king.

9. If a claim is raised by a clergyman against a layman, or by a layman against a clergyman, with regard to any tenement which the clergyman wishes to treat as free alms, but which the layman [wishes to treat] as a lay fee, let it, by the consideration of the king's chief justice and in the presence of the said justice, be settled through the recognition of twelve lawful men whether the tenement belongs to free alms or to lay fee. And if it is recognized as belonging to free alms, the plea shall be [held] in the ecclesiastical court; but if [it is recognized as belonging] to lay fee, unless both call upon the same bishop or [other] baron, the plea shall be [held] in the king's court. But if, with regard to that fee, both call upon the same bishop or [other] baron, the plea shall be [held] in the king's court. But if, with regard to that fee, both call upon the same bishop or [other] baron, the plea shall be [held] in his court; [yet] so that, on account of the recognition which has been made, he who first was seised [of the land] shall not lose his seisin until proof [of the title] has been made in the plea.

10. If any one in a city, castle, borough, or demesne manor of the lord king is summoned by an archdeacon or a bishop for some offence on account of which he ought to respond to the said persons, and if he refuses satisfaction on their summons, he may

well be placed under an interdict; but he should not be excommunicated until the chief minister of the lord king in that vill has been called upon to bring him to justice, so that he may come for satisfaction. And if the king's minister defaults in the matter, he shall be in the mercy of the lord king, and the bishop may then coerce that accused man through ecclesiastical justice.

11. Archbishops, bishops, and all parsons of the realm who hold of the king in chief have their possessions of the king as baronies and are answerable for them to the king's justices and ministers; also they follow and observe all royal laws and customs, and like other barons they should take part with the barons in the judgments of the lord king's court, until the judgment involves death or maiming.

12. When an archbishopric, bishopric, abbey, or priory within the king's gift becomes vacant, it should be in his hands; and he shall thence take all revenues and income just as from his own demesne. And when it comes to providing for the church, the lord king should summon the greater parsons of the church, and the election should be held in the king's own chapel by the assent of the lord king and by the counsel of those parsons of the kingdom whom he has called for that purpose. And there the man elected should, before being consecrated, perform homage and fealty to the lord king as to his liege lord, for life and limbs and earthly honour, saving the rights of his order.

13. If any of the magnates of the realm forcibly prevent an archbishop, bishop, or archdeacon from administering justice, either by himself or through his men, the lord king should bring them to justice. And if perchance any forcibly prevent the lord king from [administering] his justice, the archbishops, bishops, and archdeacons should bring them to justice, so that they may satisfy the lord king.

14. Chattels of those who have incurred royal forfeiture should not be withheld in any church or churchyard against the king's justice; for they are the king's own, whether they are found inside churches or outside them.

15. Pleas of debt, owed under pledge of faith or without pledge of faith, belong to the king's justice.

16. Sons of peasants should not be ordained without the assent of the lord on whose land they are known to have been born.

Now the [present] record of the aforesaid royal rights and customs was made at Clarendon by the archbishops, bishops, earls, and barons, and by the more noble and venerable men of the realm, on the fourth day before the Purification of the Blessed Virgin Mary, in the presence of the lord Henry, together with his father, the lord king. There are, moreover, other rights and customs, both many and great, of the Holy Mother Church, of the lord king, and of the barons of the realm, which are not contained in this writing; they are to be saved to Holy Church, to the lord king and his heirs, and to the barons of the realm, are inviolably to be observed forever.

2   *Roger of Hoveden*
The Annuals

Among the important English historians of the twelfth century was Roger of Hoveden, whose career spanned much of Henry II's reign. A native of Yorkshire in the north of England, Roger had access to documents, letters, and charters; he also drew heavily and almost literally from the official account entitled Gesta Regis Henrici *(Deeds of King Henry) for a significant part of the reign. One of the great values of the work, compensating for other weaknesses, is the presence of documentary materials.*

Roger's account shows, understandably, the contemporary sympathy with the archbishop as victim of the violent attack by assassins. His total acceptance of the alleged miracles that rapidly led to the martyr's sainthood should not be construed as ignorance or superstition. The description of a person whose life "was perfectly unimpeachable before God and man" was in the usual tradition of hagiography, and here a serious writer reported in all honesty accounts of water turning to wine, of Becket's appearance many miles from the location of his body, and of his performances of a benediction after his death.

SOURCE. Selections from Roger of Hoveden, *The Annals,* translated by Henry T. Riley, London: H. G. Bohn, 1853, Vol. I, pp. 258–261, 331–333, 337–338.

In the same year, a great dissension arose between the king of England and Thomas, archbishop of Canterbury, relative to the ecclesiastical dignities, which the said king of the English was attempting to disturb and lower in estimation, whereas the archbishop endeavoured by every possible means to keep the ecclesiastical power and dignities intact. For it was the king's wish that if priests, deacons, subdeacons, and other rulers of the church should be apprehended on the commission of theft, or murder, or felony, or arson, or the like crimes, they should be taken before secular judges, and punished like the laity. Against this the archbishop of Canterbury urged, that if a clerk in holy orders, or any other ruler of the Church, should be charged upon any matter, he ought to be tried by ecclesiastics and in the ecclesiastical courts; and if he should be convicted, that then he ought to be deprived of his orders, and that, when thus stripped of his office and his ecclesiastical preferment, if he should offend again, he ought to be tried at the pleasure of the king and of his deputies.

In the year of grace 1164, being the tenth year of the reign of king Henry, son of the empress Matilda, the said Henry gave to Henry, duke of Saxony, his daughter Matilda in marriage. In the same year, having called together a great council, and all the archbishops and bishops of England being assembled in his presence, he requested them, out of their love for and obedience to him, and for the establishment of the kingdom, to receive the laws of King Henry, his grandfather, and faithfully to observe them: on which Thomas, archbishop of Canterbury made answer for himself and the others, that they would receive those laws which the king said were made by his grandfather, and with good faith would observe the same; saving their orders and the honour of God and of the Holy Church in all respects. But this reservation greatly displeased the king, and he used every possible method to make the bishops promise that they would, without any exception whatever, observe those laws; to this, however, the archbishop of Canterbury would on no account agree.

A considerable time after this, Ernulph, bishop of Lisieux, came over to England, and anxiously endeavoured, day and night, to make peace between the king and the archbishop, but was unable to ensure complete success. Upon this, by the advice of the bishop of Lisieux, the king separated Roger, archbishop of

York, Robert Melun, bishop of Hereford, Robert, bishop of Lincoln, and some other prelates of the church, from the society and counsel of the archbishop of Canterbury, in order that through them he might more easily induce the archbishop to yield to his own attempts. After this, there came to England a certain man belonging to the religious orders, named Philip de Elcemosyna, being sent as legate "a latere," by Alexander the Supreme Pontiff, and all the cardinals, for the purpose of making peace between the king and archbishop of Canterbury; by whom the pope and all the cardinals sent word to the archbishop of Canterbury, that he must make peace with the king of England his master, and promise, without any exception, to obey his laws. Assenting therefore to this and other advice on the part of these great men, the archbishop of Canterbury came to the king at Woodstock, and there made a promise to the king and agreed that he would in good faith, and without any bad intent observe his laws.

Shortly after this, the clergy and people of the kingdom being convened at Clarendon, the archbishop repented that he had made this concession to the king, and, wishing to recede from his agreement, said that in making the concession he had greatly sinned, but would sin no longer in so doing. In consequence of this, the king's anger was greatly aroused against him, and he threatened him and his people with exile and death; upon which, the bishops of Salisbury and Norwich came to the archbishop, together with Robert, earl of Leicester, Reginald, earl of Cornwall, and the two Templars, Richard de Hastings and Tostes de Saint Omer, and in tears threw themselves at the feet of the archbishop, and begged that he would observe his laws. The archbishop being consequently overcome by the entreaties of such great men, came to the king, and in the presence of the clergy and the people, said that he had acceded to those laws which the king called those of his grandfather. He also conceded that the bishops should receive those laws and promise to observe them. Upon this, the king gave orders to all the earls and barons of the realm, that they should go out and call to remembrance the laws of King Henry his grandfather, and reduce them to writing. When this had been done, the king commanded the archbishops and bishops to annex their seals to the said writing; but, while the others were ready so to do, the archbishop of Canterbury swore that he would never annex his seal to that writing or confirm those laws.

When the king saw that he could not by these means attain his object, he ordered a written copy of these laws to be made, and gave a duplicate of it to the archbishop of Canterbury, which he, in spite of the prohibition of the whole of the clergy, received from the king's hand, and turning to the clergy, exclaimed, "Courage, brethren! by means of this writing we shall be enabled to discover the evil intentions of the king, and against whom we ought to be on our guard!" After which he retired from the court, and was unable by any means to recover the king's favour. And because he had acted unadvisedly in this matter, he suspended himself from the celebration of divine service from that hour, until such time as he, himself, or his messenger, should have spoken thereon with our lord the pope.

After this, there came to England Rotrod, archbishop of Rouen, on behalf of our lord the pope, for the purpose of effecting a reconciliation between the king and the archbishop of Canterbury; to which, however, the king would on no account consent, unless our lord the pope should, by his bull, confirm those laws. When this could be in nowise effected, the king sent John of Oxford and Geoffrey Riddel, his clerks, to the pope Alexander, requesting him to give the legateship of the whole of England to Roger, that archbishop of York, that so through his means he might be able to confound the archbishop of Canterbury. But our lord the pope would not, as this part of it, listen to the king's request. However, upon the petition of the king's clerks, our lord the pope conceded that the king himself should be legate for the whole of England; on such terms however, that he could do nothing offensive to the archbishop of Canterbury. The king, on seeing this, in his indignation sent back to our lord the pope the letters appointing him legate, which John of Oxford and Geoffrey Riddel had brought. . . . Thereupon, at the commencement of the seventh year of his banishment, when he was now beloved by God and sanctified by spiritual exercises, he hastened with all speed to return to his see. For the pious father was unwilling any longer to leave the church of Canterbury desolate; or else it was, because, as some believe, he has seen in the spirit the glories of his contest drawing to a close, or through a fear that, by dying elsewhere, he might be depriving his own see of the honor of his martyrdom.

As for his life, it was perfectly unimpeachable before God and man. To arise before daybreak did not seem to him a vain thing, as he knew that the Lord has promised a crown to the watchful. For every day he arose before daybreak, while all the rest were asleep, and entering his oratory would awake his chaplains and clerks from their slumbers, and, the matins and the hours of the day being chaunted, devoutly celebrate the mass; and every day and night he received three or five flagellations from the hand of a priest. After the celebration of the mass, every day he re-entered his oratory, and, shutting the door after him, devoted himself to prayer with abundant tears; and no one but God alone knew the manner in which he afflicted his flesh. And thus did he do daily unto his flesh until the hour for dining, unless some unusual solemnity or remarkable cause prevented it. On coming forth from his oratory he would come to dine among his people, not that he might sate his body with costly food, but that he might make his household cheerful thereby, and that he might fill the poor ones of the Lord with good things, whom, according to his means, he daily increased in numbers. And although costly and exquisite food and drink were set before him, still, his only food and drink were bread and water.

One day, while the archbishop was sitting at the table of Alexander, the Supreme Pontiff, a person who was aware of this secret, placed before him a cup full of water. On the Supreme Pontiff taking it up, and tasting it, he found it to be the purest wine, and delicious to drink; on which he said: "I thought that this was water;" and on replacing the cup before the archbishop, the wine immediately returned to its former taste of water. Oh wondrous change by the right hand of the Most High! Every day, when the archbishop arose from dinner, unless more important business prevented him, he always devoted himself to reading the Scriptures until the hour of vespers, at the time of sunset. His bed was covered with soft coverlets and cloths of silk, embroidered on the surface with gold wrought therein; and while other persons were asleep, he alone used to lie on the bare floor before his bed, repeating psalms and hymns, and never ceasing from prayers, until at last, overcome with fatigue, he would gradually recline his head upon a stone put beneath it in place of a pillow: and thus would his eyes enjoy sleep while his heart was ever watchful for the Lord. His inner garment was of course sackcloth made of goats' hair; with which his whole body was covered from the arms down to the knees. But his outer garments were remarkable for their splendour and extreme costliness, to the end that, thus deceiving human eyes, he might please the sight of God. There was no individual acquainted with this secret of his way of living, with the exception of two—one of whom was Robert, canon of Merton, his chaplain, and the name of the other was Brun, who had charge of his sackcloth garments, and washed them when necessary; and they were bound by their words and oaths that, during his life, they would disclose these facts to no one. . . .

Accordingly, again was this champion of Christ afflicted with injuries and hardships still more atrocious, beyond measure and number, and, by public proclamation, enjoined not to go beyond the limits of his church. Whoever showed to him, or to any one of his household, a cheerful countenance, was held to be a public enemy. However, all these things the man of God endured with great patience, and staying among those of his own household, edified them all with his conversation and with words of exhortation: and once more the archbishop took his seat in his church, fearless, and awaiting the hour at which he should receive from God the crown of martyrdom. For, being warned by many beforehand, he knew that his life would be but short, and that death was at the gates. . . .

Thus it was that, at the beginning of the seventh year of his exile, the above-named martyr Thomas struggled even unto the death for the love of God and the liberties of the Church, which had almost entirely perished as regards the English Church. He did not stand in fear of the words of the unrighteous; but having his foundation upon a firm rock, that is, upon Christ, for the name of Christ, and in the Church of Christ, by the swords of the wicked, on the fifth day of the Nativity of our Lord, being the day after Innocents's day, he himself an innocent, died. His innocent life and his death, as being precious in the eyes of God, innumerable miracles deservedly bespeak, which, not only in the place where he rested, but in divers nations and kingdoms, were wondrously shown.

On the same day the passion of the blessed Thomas was revealed by the Holy Ghost to the blessed Godric, the anchorite, at Finchale, a place which is distant from Canterbury more than a hundred and sixty miles. The monks of the church of Canterbury, on this, shut the doors of the church, and so the church remained with the celebration of the mass suspended for nearly a whole year, until they had received a reconciliation of the church from our lord the pope Alexander. But the monks took up the body of their martyr, and the first night placed it in the choir, performing around it the service for the dead. It is also said, and with truthfulness, that when they had completed around the body the obsequies of mortality, and while he was lying on the bier in the choir, about daybreak he raised his left hand and gave them the benediction; after which, they buried him in the crypt.

3   *William of Newburgh*
          History

One twelfth-century historian, William of Newburgh, was clearly distinct from those who kept brief and uncritical chronicles of year-by-year events. The independence of William's narrative is particularly clear when he discusses the Becket affair. Writing after Becket's death, when it was uniformly popular to praise the martyred saint, William did not hesitate to express his disapproval of Becket's imprudence nor to condemn the rash actions of the king. The author died shortly before 1200, and it is conjectured that he wrote his history in the last few years of his life. While much of it is neither original nor immune from error, it is a work of great value for the middle years of Henry II's reign. A comparison of William's account

SOURCE. Selections from William of Newburgh, *History of England*, from *Church Historians of England*, translated and edited by Joseph Stevenson, London: S. Beeley's, 1856, pp. 465–467, 478–482.

with Roger of Hoveden's will show certain differences in style and viewpoint.

William ventures to suggest moderately that "the blessed pope Gregory [VII] . . . would have acted with more mildness" than Thomas, and that clergy who were "guilty of heinous crimes" did not deserve the kind of legal protection the bishops, led by Thomas, demanded.

Before the year had expired in which the council was held, the displeasure of the king of England waxed hot against the venerable Thomas, archbishop of Canterbury, the unhappy source of the numerous and excessive evils which ensued. This Thomas was born in London; he was a man of acute understanding and competent eloquence as well as elegant in person and manner; he was second to none in despatch of business; he had been conspicuous in the service of Theobald, archbishop of Canterbury, and had received from him the archdeaconry of Canterbury, on the promotion of Roger to the see of York. But when Henry the second, on the demise of Stephen, (as it has been before observed,) succeeded to his hereditary kingdom, he was unwilling to be without the services of a man fit to stand before kings, so he made Becket his royal chancellor. Being elevated to this office, he executed it with such reputation, and gained at the same time such high regard and distinctions from his prince, that he seemed to share the government with him. Some years had elapsed in his secular services, when, behold, he was enlisted in ecclesiastical warfare, and obtained, through the royal pleasure, the see of Canterbury. After a time, considering piously and sagaciously the responsibility of so high an honour, he on a sudden exhibited such a change in his habit and manners, that some observed, "This is the finger of God," and others, "This is a change effected by the hand of the Most High." In the second year after his advancement, he was present at the council of Tours, where, as it is reported, being pricked by remorse of conscience, he privately resigned into the pope's hands the primacy, having, as it were, received it not regularly and canonically, but by the agency and hand of the king. The pope, approving of the transaction, restored to him his pastoral office by virtue of his ecclesiastical power, and healed the wounded conscience of the scrupulous prelate. The bishops having returned from the council to their several sees, the royal and the priestly powers began to be at variance in England, and no small commotion arose concerning the prerogatives of the clergy. For it was intimated by the judges to the king, (who was diligently occupied in the concerns of the state, and who had ordered all malefactors to be indiscriminately banished,) that many crimes against public order, such as thefts, rapines, and murders, were repeatedly committed by the clergy, to whom the correction of lay jurisdiction could not be extended. Finally, it was declared, in his presence, that during his reign more than a hundred murders had been committed by the clergy in England alone. Hereupon the king waxing extremely indignant, enacted laws, in the heat of his passion, against ecclesiastical delinquents, wherein he gave evidence of his zeal for public justice, though his severity rather exceeded the bounds of moderation. Still, however, the blame and the origin of the king's excess in this point attaches only to the prelates of our times, inasmuch as it proceeded entirely from them. For since the sacred canons enjoin that not only flagitious clerks, that is, such as are guilty of heinous crimes, but even such as are only slightly criminal, shall be degraded—and the church of England contains many thousands such, like the chaff innumerable amid the few grains of corn—what number of the clergy have there been deprived of this office during many years in England? The bishops, however, while anxious rather to maintain the liberties or rights of the clergy than to correct and root out their vices, suppose that they do God service, and the church also, by defending against established law those abandoned clergy, whom they either refuse or neglect to restrain, as their office enjoins, by the vigour of canonical censure. Hence the clergy, who, called into the inheritance of the Lord, ought to shine on earth, in their lives and conversation, like stars placed in the firmament of heaven, yet take licence and liberty to do what they please with impunity; and regard neither God, whose vengeance seems to sleep, nor men who are placed in authority; more especially as episcopal vigilance is relaxed with respect to them, while the prerogative of holy orders exempts them from all secular jurisdiction.

Thus, when the king had enacted certain statutes against the chaff of the holy order, that is to say, for the examination or punishment of the guilty clergy, in which perhaps (as it has been said) he exceeded the bounds of moderation, he conceived that they would be fully ratified could they be confirmed by the consent of the bishops. Therefore, having assembled the prelates, to procure their sanction by any means whatsoever, he so allured the whole of them with the exception of one, by blandishments, or terrified them with alarms, that they deemed it necessary to yield to and obey the royal pleasure, and set their seals to the enactment of these new constitutions—I say, with the exception of one, for the archbishop of Canterbury was alone inflexible, and remained unshaken by every assault. Upon this, the king's fury became more vehemently incensed against him, in proportion as he appeared more indebted to the royal munificence for what had been given and received. Hence the king became hostile to him, and, seeking every occasion to attack him, demanded an account of everything he had formerly done in the kingdom, in his office as chancellor. The archbishop, with intrepid freedom, replied, that having discharged his secular duties, he had been completely transferred to the church by the prince in whose service he had been engaged, and that matters of bygone date ought not to be urged against him, but this more for a pretext than for truth. While the causes of the king's anger became daily more aggravated, on the day when the archbishop was to answer at large to the allegations against him, he ordered the solemn of-fice of St. Stephen—"The princes sat and spake against me, and sinners persecuted me"—to be duly chanted before him at the celebration of mass. Afterwards he entered the court, carrying in his hand the silver cross, which was usually borne before him; and when some of the bishops present wished to undertake the office of carrying the cross before their metropolitan, he refused, and, although entreated, he would not allow any other to bear the cross in that public assembly. The king, being already en-raged beyond measure at these circumstances, had an additional incentive to his fury; for in the following night the archbishop secretly escaped, and passed beyond the sea, where, being hon-ourably received by the king, the nobility, and the bishops of France, he took up his residence for a time. The king of England, consequently, was furiously enraged at his absence; and, giving way to unbridled passion more than became a king, took an unbecoming and pitiful kind of revenge, by banishing all the archbishop's relations out of England. Now, though many persons indeed generally, led by fond affection, but little prudence, do approve everything done by those whom they love and commend, yet I by no means deem that these actions of this venerable man are worthy of commendation, however they might proceed from laudable zeal—because no benefit would result therefrom, and they only the more inflamed the royal anger, and melancholy results are known to have ensued from them—any more than I commend the actions of the blessed prince of the apostles, now at the summit of apostolical eminence, in compelling the Gentiles to Judaise after his own example, in which the teacher of the Gentiles declares him to have been reprehensible, though it is manifest that he did it from motives of laudable piety. . . .

In the year one thousand one hundred and seventy from the delivery of the Virgin, which was the seventeenth of the reign of Henry the second, the king caused his son Henry, yet a youth, to be solemnly anointed and crowned king at London, by the hands of Roger, archbishop of York. For the king not being yet appeased, the venerable Thomas, archbishop of Canterbury, was still an exile in France, though the Roman pontiff and the king of France had interested themselves extremely to bring about a reconciliation. The moment Thomas heard of this transaction, jealous for his church, he quickly informed the pope of it (by whose favour and countenance he was supported), alleging that this had taken place to the prejudice of himself and his see: and he obtained letters of severe rebuke, for the purpose of correcting equally the archbishop of York, who had performed the office in another's province, and the bishops, who, by their presence, had sanctioned it. The king, however, continued but a short time in England after the coronation of his son, and went beyond sea; and when urged by the frequent admonitions of the pope, and the earnest entreaties of the illustrious king of France, that he would, at least, condescend to be reconciled to the dignified exile, after a seven years' banishment, he at length yielded; and a solemn reconciliation took place between them, which was the more desired and the more grateful in proportion to the time of its protraction. While the king, therefore, continued abroad, the archbishop, by royal grant and permission, returned to his diocese; having in his possession, unknown to the king, letters obtained from the pope against the archbishop of York, and the other prelates who had assisted at that most unfortunate coronation; which was the means of breaking the recently concluded peace, and had become the incentive to greater rage. These letters, for the suspension of the prelates, preceded him into England; and he followed them himself, burning with zeal for justice, but God knows whether altogether according to knowledge; but it is not allowed to my insignificance, by any means, to judge hastily of the actions of so great a man. I think, nevertheless, that the blessed pope Gregory, during the slight and yet fresh reconciliation of the king would have acted with more mildness, and would have deemed it proper, (considering the time and terms of their reunion,) to have winked at things, which might have been endured without injury to the christian faith, according to the language of the prophet, "The prudent shall keep silence at that time; for it is an evil time." Therefore, what was done by the venerable pontiff at this juncture, I neither think worthy of commendation, nor do I presume to censure; but this I say, that, if this holy man, through rather too great a fervency of zeal, was guilty of some little excess, yet was it all purged out in the fire of that holy suffering which is known to have ensued. Therefore, although holy men are to be loved and commended by us, who are so sensible of our great inferiority, still we are not bound to love or praise them for actions, in which they either do, or have shown the weakness of their human nature; but merely, for such as we are bound implicitly to imitate. For who can say that they should be imitated in all thing—when the apostle James asserts, "that in many things we offend all?" Wherefore, they are to be applauded, not in all their actions, but with prudence and caution, that God's prerogative may be kept inviolate, in whose praises, indeed, none can exceed, how much soever he may attempt it.

The bishops, on account of the offence before mentioned (which I could wish to have remained unnoticed at the time), being suspended, at the instance of the venerable Thomas, from all episcopal functions, by the authority of the apostolic see, the king was exasperated by the complaints of some of them, and grew angry and indignant beyond measure, and losing the mastery of himself, in the heat of his exuberant passion, from the abundance of his perturbed spirit, poured forth the language of indiscretion. On which, four of the bystanders, men of noble race and renowned in arms, wrought themselves up to the commission of iniquity through zeal for their earthly master; and leaving the royal presence, and crossing the sea, with as much haste as if posting to a solemn banquet, and urged on by the fury they had imbibed, they arrived at Canterbury on the fifth day after Christmas, where they found the venerable archbishop occupied in the celebration of that holy festival with religious joy. Proceeding to him just as he had dined, and was sitting with certain honourable personages, omitting even to salute him, and holding forth the terror of the king's name, they commanded (rather than asked, or admonished him) forthwith to remit the suspension of the prelates who had obeyed the king's pleasure, to whose contempt and disgrace this act redounded. On his replying that the sentence of a higher power was not to be abrogated by an inferior one, and that it was not his concern to pardon persons suspended not by himself, but by the Roman pontiff, they had recourse to violent threats. Undismayed at these words, though uttered by men raging and extremely exasperated, he spoke with singular freedom and confidence. In consequence, becoming more enraged than before, they hastily retired, and bringing their arms, (for they had entered without them,) they prepared themselves, with loud clamour and indignation, for the commission of a most atrocious crime. The venerable prelate was persuaded by his friends to avoid the madness of these furious savages, by retiring into the holy church. When, from his determination to brave every danger, he did not acquiesce, on the forcible and tumultuous approach of his enemies, he was at length dragged by the friendly violence of his associates to the protection of the holy church. The monks were solemnly chanting vespers to Almighty God, as he entered the sacred temple of Christ, shortly to become an evening sacrifice. The servants of Satan pursued having neither respect as Christians to his holy order, nor to the sacred place, or season; but attacking the dignified prelate as he stood in prayer before the holy altar, even during the festival of Christmas, these truly nefarious Christians most inhumanly murdered him. Having done the deed, and retiring as if triumphant, they departed with unhallowed joy. Recollecting, however, that perhaps the transaction might displease the person in whose behalf they had been so zealous, they retired to the northern parts of England, waiting until they could fully discover the disposition of their monarch towards them.

The frequent miracles which ensued manifested how precious, in the sight of God, was the death of the blessed prelate, and how great the atrocity of the crime committed against him, in the circumstances of time, place, and person. Indeed, the report of such a dreadful outrage, quickly pervading every district of the western world, sullied the illustrious king of England, and so obscured his fair fame among Christian potentates, that, as it could scarcely be credited to have been perpetrated without his consent and mandate, he was assailed by the execrations of almost all, and deemed fit to be the object of general detestation. Upon hearing of this transaction of his adherents, and learning the stain cast by them upon his glory, and the almost indelible brand on his character, he was so grieved, that, it is related, for several days he tasted nothing. For, whether he should pardon those murderers or not, he was sensible that people would be inclined to think evil of him. Moreover, should he spare these nefarious wretches, he would seem to have lent either daring or authority to such a crime; but, should he punish them for what they were supposed to have done not without his command, he would, on every hand, be most flagitious. In consequence, he thought it best to pardon them; and regarding equally his own credit and their salvation, he ordered them to be presented to the holy see, to undergo a solemn penance. This was done accordingly; and they, wounded in conscience, proceeded to Rome, and by the sovereign pope were ordered, by way of penance, to go to Jerusalem; where, as it is said, they all closed their lives, signally executing the appointed measure of their atonement; but of this hereafter.

Whilst almost all persons then attributed the death of this holy man to the king, and more especially the French nobles, who had been jealous of his good fortune, were instigating the apostolical see against him, as the true and undoubted author of this great enormity, the king sent representatives to Rome, to mitigate, by submissive entreaty, the displeasure which was raging against him. When they arrived at Rome, (as all men joined in execrating the king *of* England,) it was with difficulty that they were admitted. Constantly affirming, however, that this dreadful outrage was not committed either by the command or concurrence of their master, they, at length, obtained, that legates *a latere* from the pope, vested with full power, should be sent into France, who, on carefully investigating, and ascertaining the truth of the matter, should admit the king either to the purgation of his fame, or punish him, if found guilty, by ecclesiastical censure, which was done accordingly. For two cardinals being despatched from the holy see—that is to say, the venerable Albert, who afterwards presided over it, and Theodinus—they arrived in France; and a solemn meeting being summoned in the territory of the king of England, consisting of prelates and nobles, they formally undertook the purgation of this same prince; there, humbly making his appearance, and firmly protesting that what had sullied his fame had taken place without his wish or command, and that he had never been so much afflicted with any transaction before. Indeed, he did not deny that those murderers had, perhaps, taken occasion and daring to their excessive fury from some words of his too incautiously uttered; when, hearing of the suspension of the prelates, he became infuriated, and spake unadvisedly. "And on this account," said he, "I do not refuse the discipline of the Church: I will submit devotedly to whatever you decree, and I will fulfill your injunction." Saying this, and casting off his clothes, after the custom of public penitents, he submitted himself naked to ecclesiastical discipline. The cardinals, overjoyed at the humility of so great a prince, and weeping with joy, while numbers joined their tears, and gave praise to God, dissolved the assembly—the king's conscience being quieted, and his character in some measure restored. Richard, prior of Dover, then succeeded the blessed Thomas in the see of Canterbury.

4   *Letters, Alexander III to Thomas Becket*

Pope Alexander III used diplomatically cautious moderation to pre-
vent the two antagonists from sustaining an incurable rupture. He
dared not let the clergy think he was deserting their cause; he dared
not provoke the king into supporting a rival pope. The two letters
quoted here illustrate his quandary. In the first, Alexander overrules
a judgment against Becket, arguing that the king and his barons could
not remove goods that the archbishop did not have. In the second
letter the pope begs the archbishop to proceed cautiously and not
to precipitate an open breach with the king. Alexander, a product
of the new legal learning of his age, appeals to the judgment of law
as well as to the expediency of diplomacy.

Letter written from Clermont, June 1165, by Pope Alexander
III to Thomas Becket.

That the less cannot judge the greater, and especially him to
whom he is known to be subject by right of prelacy and is held
bound by the chain of obedience, is declared by laws both human
and divine, and is set forth with particular clarity in the statutes of
the holy fathers. Accordingly we, whose province it is to correct
errors of judgment and to amend those things which, if not corrected, would leave a pernicious example to posterity, and, having
pondered these matters with anxious care, and considering that
through the fault of one man the Church ought not to sustain
hurt or loss, we adjudge the sentence presumptuously passed
against you by the bishops and barons of England on the ground
that you did not obey the king's first summons—in which sentence the said bishops and barons adjudged a forfeiture of all
your movables contrary both to the form of law and ecclesi-

SOURCE. From *English Historical Documents*, Vol. II, 1042–1189, edited
by David C. Douglas and George W. Greenaway, New York: Oxford
University Press, 1953, p. 742. Reprinted by permission of Oxford University Press, and Eyre and Spottiswoode, Ltd.

astical custom, especially since you have no movables save the goods of your church—to be utterly void, and we quash the same by apostolic authority, ordering that for the future it shall have no force, and avail nothing to bring prejudice or hurt hereafter to you or your successors or to the church committed to your governance.

Letter written also from Clermont, June 1165, Alexander III to Thomas Becket.

Since the days are evil and many things must be endured through the nature of the times, we beg you to be discreet, and we warn, advise and exhort you to show yourself wary, prudent, and circumspect in all your actions for your own sake and that of the Church. Do nothing hastily or precipitately, but act with gravity and deliberation by every means at your disposal, with a view to recovering the favour and good will of the illustrious king of the English, so far as is consistent with the liberty of the Church and the dignity of your office. Forbear with the king until the following Easter, and study to avoid taking any measure against him or his realm until the prescribed date. For by then God will vouchsafe better days, and both you and we may safely proceed further in this matter.

5   *Letters from Thomas Becket*

From Roger of Hoveden's history, a portion of which is quoted above, come the next two letters. The archbishop addressed one to all of the bishops directly subject to him, his suffragan bishops. In it he announced the excommunication of two who, on behalf of the king, approached the antipope, Reginald of Cologne, to explore the possibility of supporting him if Alexander III proved recalcitrant. Becket also excommunicated those who took advantage of his exile to profit from church lands in the Canterbury diocese, including Ranulph de

SOURCE. Roger of Hoveden, *The Annals*, translated by Henry T. Riley, London: H. G. Bohn, 1853, pp. 275–278, 312–313.

Broc, whose name is mentioned in other selections as one of those who continued to be a bitter enemy of the archbishop to the very end. Becket threatened to excommunicate the king, but refrained from carrying out the threat.

The second letter concerns Becket's most consistent opponent among the clergy, Gilbert Foliot, whose excommunication the archbishop here announces.

1166, LETTER FROM ARCHBISHOP THOMAS BECKET TO HIS SUFFRAGAN BISHOPS

Thomas, by the grace of God, the humble servant of the chuch of Canterbury, to his venerable brethren, the bishop of London, and the other bishops of the whole province of Canterbury; may they so enjoy temporal blessings, as not to lose those of eternity. My most dearly-beloved brethren, wherefore do ye not arise with me against my enemies? Why do ye not take part with me against those who work iniquity? Is it that ye are ignorant that the Lord scattereth abroad the bones of those who please men? They shall be confounded, inasmuch as the Lord hath despised them. Your discreetness well knows that when the errors of a man are not opposed, they are approved; and that when truth is not defended, it is smothered. He, too, who does not hasten to the reproval of that which ought to be corrected, appears, Saint Gregory giving his testimony thereto, to encourage him who commits the wrong. Enough, and even more than enough, have we put up with our lord, the king of England; and yet, in return, the Church of God has received no support from him. We hold that it is a thing dangerous and not to be endured, to leave unpunished for the future, as hitherto, the excessive outrages committed by him and his officials against the Church of God and the ministers of that Church; and the more especially so, inasmuch as, most frequently by letters and messages, and other means, as was our duty, we have endeavored to recall him from the perverseness of his course. But since we have been hardly heard by him, much more listened to, after invoking the grace of the Holy Spirit, we have publicly condemned, and have made null and void that writing in which are contained, not those customs, but rather those corruptions by which at the present time the Church of England is disturbed and put to confusion, as also the authority of the said writing. All who observe, or enforce, or counsel, or aid, or defend the same, we do likewise excommunicate; and all you bishops, by the authority of God and of ourselves, we do absolve from the promises, by which, against the rules of the Church, you bound yourselves to the observance thereof. For who is there that can doubt that the priests of Christ are appointed to be the fathers and masters of kings and princes, and of all the faithful? Is it not understood to be an act of lamentable madness for the son to attempt to make his father, or the disciple his master, obedient to him, and by unrighteous means of compulsion to render him subject to his power? One, too, whom he believes to have power to bind and to loose him not only on earth, but even in heaven as well? Therefore, in order that we may not fall into the commission of this error, we have rendered of no effect, and have made null and void the authority of that writing, as also the writing itself, together with all the corruptions that are therein contained; and more especially the following: Appeal shall not in any case be made to the Apostolic See, except with the king's permission. It shall not be lawful for an archbishop or bishop to depart from the kingdom, to attend the summons of our lord the pope, without the king's permission. It shall not be lawful for a bishop to excommunicate any person who holds of the king *in capite*, or to lay an interdict upon any one of his officers, without the king's permission. It shall not be lawful for a bishop to take cognizance of perjury or breach of faith. The clergy are to be brought before secular tribunals. Laymen, whether the king or other persons, are to take cognizance of causes as to churches and tithes, and other enactments to a like effect. We do also denounce as excommunicated, and have excommunicated by name, the man called John of Oxford, who has fallen into a damnable heresy, by tendering an oath to schismatics, through whom a schism that had almost died out has revived in Germany, as also for communicating with that most notorious schismatic, Reginald of Cologne; and because, contrary to the mandate of our lord the pope and of myself, he has taken unlawful possession of the deanery of the church of Salisbury; a deed which, so detestable as it is, so contrary to right, so pernicious in its example to the

Church of God, we do make utterly null and void, and do render it of no effect whatsoever; and it is our command to the bishop of Salisbury, and the chapter of that church, in virtue of their obedience, and at the peril of their orders, on seeing this our letter, thenceforth no longer to hold him as dean thereof. In like manner, we do denounce as excommunicated, and have excommunicated, Richard de Ivechester, because he has fallen into the same damnable heresy, by holding communication with Reginald of Cologne, the schismatic, as also by inventing and contriving all kinds of mischief with those schismatics and Germans, to the destruction of the Church of God, and especially of the Church of Rome, according to the terms agreed upon between our lord the king and them. We have also excommunicated Richard de Lucy and Jocelyn de Baliol, who have been the authors and fabricators of these corruptions; also Ranulph de Broc, who has taken possession of the property of the church of Canterbury, which by right is a provision for the poor ,and witholds the same, and has arrested our men as though they were laymen, and detains them in his custody. We have also excommunicated Hugh de Saint Clair and Thomas Fitz-Bernard, who, without either connivance or consent on our part, have laid hands upon the property and possessions of the said church of Canterbury. . . . The Scripture, also, in one place, tells us that he who agrees with the sinful, and defends another in his sin, shall be accursed before God and man, and shall be visited with the most severe afflictions; and likewise, that if any one defends another in his sin, he shall be more severely corrected than he who has committed the sin. As yet indeed, we have delayed pronouncing this sentence against the person of our lord the king, in the hope that perchance, by the inspiration of the Divine grace, he may recover his senses; still, we shall very shortly pronounce it, unless he shall make haste so to do. . . . And you, brother, the bishop of London, we do command, and by virtue of our authority over you, enjoin the same, that you will disclose and show this our letter to the rest of your brethren and to all brother bishops of our province. Fare ye well in Christ, and pray continually for us.

LETTER FROM ARCHBISHOP THOMAS BECKET
TO GILBERT FOLIOT, BISHOP OF LONDON

Thomas, by the grace of God, archbishop of Canterbury, and legate of the Apostolic See, to Gilbert, bishop of London—would indeed that he could say, his brother—may he turn away from evil and do what is good. Your extravagances we have borne with, so long as we could, and we hope that our endurance and long-suffering, which have been to ourselves detrimental beyond measure, may not redound to the injury of the whole Church. But inasmuch as you have always abused our patience, and have not been willing to listen to our lord the pope or ourselves in the advice which concerned your salvation, but rather, your obstinacy has been always increasing for the worse; at length, the necessities of our duty and the requirements of the law forcing us thereto, we have, for just and manifest causes, smitten and excommunicated you with the sentence of anathema, and have cut you off from the body of Christ, which is the Church, until you make condign satisfaction. Therefore, by virtue of your obedience, and at the peril of your salvation, or your dignity and of your priestly orders, as the form of the Church prescribes, we do command you to abstain from all communion with the faithful; lest by coming in contact with you, the Lord's flock may be contaminated to its ruin, whereas it ought to be instructed by your teaching, and taught by your example how to live.

6   *Letter, Gilbert Foliot to Thomas Becket*

The bishop of London, secure in his own sense of right and solidly entrenched with the forces of the king, did not accept lightly the admonitions of his exiled archbishop. In a forceful reply, he took the offensive and attacked Becket for his vacillating leadership. The following letter states clearly the case put forward by Gilbert

SOURCE. William Fitzstephen, *The Life and Death of Thomas Becket*, edited by George W. Greenaway, published by The Folio Society for its members in 1961, pp. 113–116. Reprinted by permission of the publisher.

*Foliot. One by one it names the bishops and declares them innocent
of Becket's charges. Then Foliot puts the major blame for the crisis
upon the archbishop himself.*

. . . Let us recall to mind what took place at Clarendon, where
for three whole days the sole object was to obtain from us a
promise to observe unconditionally the customs and privileges of
the realm. We stood by you then, because we thought you were
standing courageously in the spirit of the Lord. We stood immovable and undismayed. We stood firm, to the ruin of our fortunes, ready to suffer bodily torment or exile, or, if God so
willed, even the sword. What man ever succeeded in getting
more unanimous support than you did on that occasion? We
were all shut up in one chamber, and on the third day the princes
and nobles of the realm, waxing hot in their wrath, burst into
the chamber where we sat, threw off their cloaks and shook their
fists at us, exclaiming, "Attend, all ye who set at naught the
statutes of the realm and heed not the king's commands. These
hands, these arms, yea, even our bodies are not our own, but belong to our lord the king, and they are ready at his nod to avenge
every wrong done to him and to work his will, whatever it may
be. No matter what he may command, it will be most just in our
eyes, since it proceeds from his will alone. Take fresh counsel
then and bend your minds to his command, that you may avert
the danger while yet there is time." What followed upon this?
Did anyone flee or turn tail? Was anyone broken in spirit? Your
letter reproaches us for having turned our backs in the day of
battle, for having neither advanced against the adversary nor
placed ourselves as a wall of defence before the house of the Lord.
Let God judge between us. Let him judge in whose cause we
would not bend before the threats of princes. Let Him judge who
it was that fled, and who was a deserter in the battle. Assuredly
it was not that noble prelate and most constant champion of God's
cause, Henry of Winchester, nor Nigel of Ely, nor Robert of
Lincoln, nor Hilary of Chichester, nor Jocelyn of Salisbury, nor
Bartholomew of Exeter, nor Richard of Chester, nor Roger of
Worcester, nor Robert of Hereford, nor Gilbert of London. All

these lacked not courage, but there was found none to smite them; these men accounted temporal things as dross and exposed themselves and their possessions fearlessly for Christ and His Church. Let the truth then be told; let the light of day be shed on what then occurred in the presence of us all. It was the leader of our chivalry who turned his back, the captain of our camp who fled; our lord of Canterbury himself abandoned the society of his brethren and forsook our common counsel. He made his own decision, and when he returned to us after a space, uttered these words, "It is the Lord's will that I should forswear myself; for the present I submit and incur perjury, to do penance for it later as best I may." Hearing such words, we stood thunderstruck, clinging to each other with mutual astonishment and groaning in spirit at the fall of one whom we had esteemed a paragon of virtue and constancy. There is no such thing as *yea-and-nay* with the Lord, and we did not anticipate that His disciple was so easily to be moved. When the head is faint, the other members become faint also and straightway suffer from the same weakness. Our archbishop himself acquiesced in the king's prerogative and the ancient customs of the realm, and agreed to their being recorded, and when he had himself sworn unconditionally to our lord the king "in the word of truth" to observe them for the future, he constrained us by force to bind ourselves by a similar pledge of obedience. Thus an end was put to this dispute and peace was restored between throne and priesthood.

. . . Furthermore you added to your offences, in that you fled by night in disguise, as if plots had been laid against your life and person, and after some little time you secretly escaped from the realm overseas, although no one was pursuing you or driving you into exile. You have chosen to reside for a time in a foreign land beyond your lord's jurisdiction. From thence you are now endeavouring to steer the ship of the Church, which you left without a pilot, amid the waves and storms. From thence you issue orders and exhortations to us to turn to you and find safety, to suffer death for Christ by following in your footsteps, and to fear not to hazard our souls for the liberation of the Church. . . .

All these things we have long brooded over; all this has long been the subject of our meditations. . . . If we weigh your deeds, father, and not your words only, we shall not rashly or lightly invoke martyrdom. For you bowed the knee at Clarendon and took to flight at Northampton; you lay hidden in disguise for a time and escaped secretly beyond the confines of the realm. What did you gain by this, except to show your anxiety to escape from the death with which no one threatened you? With what face then, father, do you now invite us to meet the death from which you shrank and fled, as you have shown by such manifest tokens to all the world and in the clear light of day? What kind of love is it which would urge us to take upon us the burden you have cast off? The sword hangs over us, the sword which you escaped and which you strive to ward off with missiles rather than to fight against in hand-to-hand combat. Perchance you invite us to imitate you in flight. But the sea is closed to us since your escape, and all the ships and harbours are strictly guarded. Islands are indeed a king's strongest prisons, and escape from them is well-nigh impossible. If we must fight, let it be at close quarters. If we join battle with the king, his sword will be measured with our own. If we inflict wounds on him, we must expect to receive wounds in return. Surely your annual revenues are not so great that you would wish to recover them by shedding the blood of your brethren! Even the Jews spurned the money which Judas brought back to them, because they knew it was the price of blood.

Thanks be to God, there is no dispute between us about the faith or the sacraments or morals. A right faith burns brightly in the king, the bishops and the people. The whole dispute is with the king and about the king, on account of certain customs, which he asserts were observed and maintained by his predecessors, and which he himself desires to be observed. Your Highness has admonished him to desist from his purpose, but he will not renounce what antiquity and long usage in the realm have sanctioned. This is why you have resorted to arms and have brandished the sword above his sacred and noble head. But, as has often been pointed out, he did not himself institute these customs; on the contrary, as the whole history of the kingdom bears witness, he found them already established. . . . You should have handled such matters with mature deliberation, not with the ardour of a novice. You should have sought advice from your fellow-bishops and others. You should have studied the works of the Fathers and weighed the gains of the Church against her losses. You ought not to have taken a decisive step, until it was apparent that no remedy existed, and when at last your decision was made, you should have considered, in accordance with the form of the sacred canons, against whom it was directed, for what cause and by what means, whether it was for the good of the Church, and what would be the consequences for the latter, if the step were not taken. . . .

If only the humility, which you had begun to show, had proved to be more lasting, the Church of God in this realm would have had cause for widespread rejoicing. For the goal at which you were aiming had been already gained by entreaty, but the fresh disturbance you have lately provoked has ruined everything. Those terrible letters, which you dispatched to the king, displayed neither the affection of a father nor the modesty of a bishop, and all that had been painfully secured through the admonitions of the supreme pontiff and the suppliant and earnest devotion of many others was at once ruined by your threats. So you have again gravely injured both the king and the kingdom and created a scandal worse than any which had occurred before. May God avert the issue which we dread, if this state of affairs continues: at least may it not come to this in our time!

7   *Letters from Henry II*

King Henry's letters were not lengthy and polemical as Thomas's were. They were terse, blunt, and specific. One can picture the ruddy-faced monarch dictating them in his usual haste, pacing the floor with his abundant store of energy.

The first, addressed to Louis VII, is an attempt to persuade the French king to refuse help to the exiled archbishop. This ploy, of course, failed, as Henry probably knew it would. The second is a

SOURCE. *English Historical Documents*, Vol. II, 1042–1189, edited by David C. Douglas and George W. Greenaway, New York: Oxford University Press, 1956, pp. 734–735, 741, 756. Reprinted by permission of Oxford University Press and Eyre and Spottiswoode (Publishers) Ltd.

writ to the English bishops, designed to undermine the pro-Becket faction. The last dates from the final reconciliation between Becket and the king, just before Becket returned to Canterbury from his exile.

In the third message the king addresses his son Henry, whose recent coronation by the archbishop of York had stirred up new troubles. After the reconciliation late in 1170, the king recognized the full rights of the archbishop, even though the writ insists that the settlement was "according to my will." Compare this with the first letter, where Henry refers to the fact that Becket "was archbishop of Canterbury," clearly stressing the past tense.

HENRY II TO LOUIS VII, OCTOBER 1164

To his lord and friend, Louis, illustrious king of the French, H[enry], king of the English, duke of the Normans and of the men of Aquitaine, and count of the Angevins, greeting and love. Be it known to you that Thomas, who was archbishop of Canterbury, has been publicly judged in my court by full council of the barons of my realm as a wicked and perjured traitor against me, and under the manifest name of traitor has wrongfully departed, as my messengers will tell you more fully. Wherefore I earnestly beg you not to permit a man guilty of such infamous crimes and treasons, or his men, to remain in your realm. Let not this great enemy of mine, so it please you, have any counsel or aid from you and yours, even as I would not give any such help myself to your enemies in my realm, nor would I allow it to be given. Rather if it please you, help me to take vengeance on my great enemy for this insult, and seek my honour, even as you would wish me to do for you if there were need of it. Witness Robert, earl of Leicester. At Northampton.

HENRY II TO THE BISHOPS OF ENGLAND, DECEMBER 1164

You know with what malice Thomas, archbishop of Canterbury, has acted towards me and my kingdom, and how basely he has fled. I therefore command you that his clerks, who were with him after his flight, and the other clerks, who have disparaged my honour and the honour of the realm shall not receive any of the revenues which they have within your bishopric except by my order. Witness: Richard of Lucé. At Marlborough.

WRIT OF HENRY II, OCTOBER 1170

Henry, king of England, to his son, Henry the king, greeting. Know that Thomas, archbishop of Canterbury, has made peace with me according to my will. I therefore command that he and all his men shall have peace. You are to ensure that the archbishop and all his men who left England for his sake shall have all their possessions as they had them three months before the archbishop withdrew from England. Moreover, you will cause to come before you the senior and more important knights of the honour of Saltwood, and by their oath you will cause recognition to be made of what is held there in fee from the archbishopric of Canterbury; and what the recognition shall declare to be in the fief of the archbishop you will cause him to have. Witness: Rotrou, archbishop of Rouen. At Chinon.

8   *John of Salisbury*
                              Policraticus

John of Salisbury, a brilliant scholar who, like Thomas Becket, had studied in Paris and had immersed himself in the newly expanding doctrines of canon law, was a friend and close supporter of the archbishop. Along with Becket he had served on the staff of Theobald, archbishop of Canterbury, until Theobald's death in 1161.

In his essay Policraticus, *John developed a carefully reasoned case for his claim that the church held precedence over the crown. John*

SOURCE. *The Statesman's Book of John of Salisbury*, translated and edited by John Dickinson. Copyright, 1927, 1955, pp. 9–14. Reprinted by permission of Appleton-Century-Crofts, Educational Division, Meredith Corporation.

*wrote the long study, dedicating it to Becket, and presented it to him
while Becket was still chancellor. Perhaps the author's hope was to
persuade the chancellor to soften the king's exercise of power; if so,
it did not influence Becket's political behavior until he had exchanged
his chancellor's robes for his clerical pallium.*

*John of Salisbury became the new archbishop's secretary, counsel-
lor, and close friend, and there is strong reason for supposing that he
influenced Thomas's shift of policy toward more militant support of
the church. In the selections below, John argues that the clergy out-
ranks royalty, that a secular official dare not undertake to punish a
clerk, and finally that a tyrannical king may be overthrown and even
killed by the society he tyrannizes.*

This sword, then, the prince receives from the hand of the
Church, although she herself has no sword of blood at all. Nevertheless she has this sword, but she uses it by the hand of the
prince, upon whom she confers the power of bodily coercion,
retaining to herself authority over spiritual things in the person
of the pontiffs. The prince is, then, as it were, a minister of the
priestly power, and one who exercises that side of the sacred
offices which seems unworthy of the hands of the priesthood.
For every office existing under, and concerned with the execution of, the sacred laws is really a religious office, but that is
inferior which consists in punishing crimes, and which therefore
seems to be typified in the person of the hangman. Wherefore
Constantine, most faithful emperor of the Romans, when he had
convoked the council of priests at Nicaea, neither dared to take
the chief place for himself nor even to sit among the presbyters,
but chose the hindmost seat. Moreover, the decrees which he
heard approved by them he reverenced as if he had seen them
emanate from the judgment-seat of the divine majesty. Even the
rolls of petitions containing accusations against priests which they
brought to him in a steady stream he took and placed in his bosom
without opening them. And after recalling them to charity and
harmony, he said that it was not permissible for him, as a man,
and one who was subject to the judgment of priests, to examine
cases touching gods, who cannot be judged save by God alone.
And the petitions which he had received he put into the fire

without even looking at them, fearing to give publicity to accu-sations and censures against the fathers, and thereby incur the curse of Cham, the undutiful son, who did not hide his father's shame. Wherefore he said, as is narrated in the writings of Nicholas the Roman pontiff, "Verily if with mine own eyes I had seen a priest of God, or any of those who wear the monastic garb, sinning, I would spread my cloak and hide him, that he might not be seen of any." Also Theodosius, the great emperor, for a merited fault, though not so grave a one, was suspended by the priest of Milan from the exercise of his regal powers and from the insignia of his imperial office, and patiently and solemnly he performed the penance for homicide which was laid upon him. Again, according to the testimony of the teacher of the gentiles, greater is he who blesses man than he who is blessed; and so he in whose hands is the authority to confer a dignity excels in honor and the privileges of honor him upon whom the dignity itself is conferred. Further, by the reasoning of the law it is his right to refuse who has the power to grant, and he who can lawfully bestow can lawfully take away. Did not Samuel pass sentence of deposition against Saul by reason of his disobedience, and supersede him on the pinnacle of kingly rule with the lowly son of Ysai? But if one who has been appointed prince has per-formed duly and faithfully the ministry which he has undertaken, as great honor and reverence are to be shown to him as the head excels in honor all the members of the body. Now he per-forms his ministry faithfully when he is mindful of his true status, and remembers that he bears the person of the *universitas* of those subject to him; and when he is fully conscious that he owes his life not to himself and his own private ends, but to others, and allots it to them accordingly, with duly ordered charity and affection. Therefore he owes the whole of himself to God, most of himself to his country, much to his relatives and friends, very little to foreigners, but still somewhat. He has duties to the very wise and the very foolish, to little children and to the aged. Supervision over these classes of persons is common to all in authority, both those who have care over spiritual things and those who exercise temporal jurisdiction. . . . And so let him be father and husband to his subjects, or, if he has known some af-fection more tender still, let him employ that; let him desire to be loved rather than feared, and show himself to them as such a man that they will out of devotion prefer his life to their own, and regard his preservation and safety as a kind of public life; and then all things will prosper well for him, and a small body-guard will, in case of need, prevail by their loyalty against innumerable adversaries. For love is strong as death; and the wedge which is held together by strands of love is not easily broken.

When the Dorians were about to fight against the Athenians they consulted the oracles regarding the outcome of the battle. The reply was that they would be victorious if they did not kill the king of the Athenians. When they went to war their soldiers were therefore enjoined above all else to care for the safety of the king. At that time the king of the Athenians was Codrus, who, learning of the response of the god and the precautions of the enemy, laid aside his royal garb and entered the camp of the enemy bearing faggots on his back. Men tried to bar his way and a disturbance arose in the course of which he was killed by a soldier whom he had struck with his pruning-hook. When the king's body was recognized, the Dorians returned home without fighting a battle. Thus the Athenians were delivered from the war by the valor of their leader, who offered himself up to death for the safety of his country. Likewise Licurgus in his reign established decrees which confirmed the people in obedience to their princes, and the princes in just principles of government; he abolished the use of gold and silver, which are the material of all wickedness, he gave to the senate guardianship over the laws and to the people the power of recruiting the senate; he decreed that virgins should be given in marriage without a dowry to the end that men might make choice of wives and not of money; he desired the greatest honor to be bestowed upon old men in proportion to their age; and verily nowhere else on earth does old age enjoy a more honored station. Then, in order to give perpetuity to his laws, he bound the city by an oath to change nothing of his laws until he should return again. He thereupon set out for Crete and lived there in perpetual exile; and when he died, he ordered his bones to be thrown into the sea for fear that if they should be taken back to Lacedaemon, they might regard themselves as absolved from the obligation of their oath in the matter of changing the laws.

BOOK III, CHAPTER 15, FROM PIKE, *FRIVOLITIES*

But on whom ought this oil of the sinner to be bestowed which the predecessor of the Kings of the faith reproves and for the purchase of which the words of the Gospel send the foolish virgins who were excluded? On him forsooth who is filthy, who by the just judgment of God is filthy still, and who strives to shine in the esteem of the vulgar rather than to glow with the fire of love and its works. Hence even in secular literature, the caution is given that one must live one way with a friend and another with a tyrant. For it is lawful to flatter him whom it is lawful to slay. Further it is not merely lawful to slay a tyrant but even right and just. He that taketh the sword is worthy of perishing with the sword. But the words *by taking the sword* refer to the one who usurps it in his temerity, not to him who receives from God the right to use it.

Especially is he who receives power from God the slave of the laws and the servant of right and justice; but he who usurps power oppresses justice, and makes the laws slaves to his own will. Therefore it is fitting that justice arm herself against him who disarms the laws, and that the power of the state treat him with severity who strives to palsy the hand of the state.

Though treason takes many forms there is none more deadly than that which is aimed against the very body of justice. The whole state has a case against tyrants, and were it possible, even more than the whole state; for if it be permissible that all prosecute those charged with treason, how much more, then, those who trample down the laws which have the right to rule over rulers themselves! Truly there will be no one to avenge a public enemy, and he who does not prosecute him sins against himself and against the whole body of the secular state.

SOURCE. Joseph B. Pike, *Frivolities of Courtiers and Footprints of Philosophers*, Minneapolis: University of Minnesota Press, 1938, pp. 211–212. Reprinted by permission of the publisher.

9

Edward Grim
"Martyrdom"

Eight different biographies of Thomas Becket have survived from the late twelfth century, and there is evidence that at least one more may have been written. Edward Grim, one of the eight writers, was present when the four knights assassinated Thomas. Unlike John of Salisbury and a few others who fled from the scene, Grim stayed and tried to hold off the knights; his own arm was nearly severed as a result.

His biography reflects a careful attempt to gather source materials and to use them judiciously, in spite of occasional reliance on hearsay and upon at least one other contemporary account. Apparently he had not known the archbishop personally, as had other biographers including William Fitzstephen, Herbert of Bosham, and John of Salisbury, until he arrived at Canterbury a few days before the fatal event that he describes here.

The work of a witness as well as a participant, Grim's account of Becket's last hour has been used repeatedly by generations of historians ever since. Milman's nineteenth century account of the same event, quoted later in this volume, draws heavily from Grim, repeating some of the direct quotations here attributed to those who were in the church at the time of the murder.

So then the aforesaid men, no knights forsooth but miserable wretches, as soon as they landed, summoned the king's officials, whom the archbishop had already excommunicated, and by falsely proclaiming that they were acting with the king's approval and in his name, they got together a band of knights and their followers. For they were easily persuaded to this crime by the knights' statement that they had come to settle the affair by order of the king. They then collected in a body, ready for any impious

SOURCE. *English Historical Documents,* Vol. II, 1042–1189, edited by David C. Douglas and George W. Greenaway, New York: Oxford University Press, 1956, pp. 761–768. Reprinted by permission of Oxford University Press, and Eyre and Spottiswoode, Ltd.

deed, and on the fifth day after the Nativity of Christ, that is, on the morrow of the Feast of the Holy Innocents, they gathered together against the innocent. The hour of dinner being over, the saint had already withdrawn with some of his household into an inner chamber to transact some business, leaving the crowd awaiting his return in the hall without. The four knights with one attendant forced their way in. They were received with respect as servants of the king and well known to the archbishop's household; and those who had waited on the archbishop, being now themselves at dinner, invited them to share their table. They scorned the offer, thirsting rather for blood than for food. By their order the archbishop was informed that four men had arrived who wished to speak with him on behalf of the King. On his giving consent, they were permitted to enter. For a long time they sat in silence and neither saluted the archbishop nor spoke to him. Nor did the man of wise counsel salute them immediately they came in, in order that, according to the Scriptures, "By thy words shalt thou be justified," he might discover their intentions from their questions. After a while, however, he turned to them and, carefully scanning the face of each, he greeted them in a friendly manner; but the unhappy wretches who had made a pact with death, straightway answered his greeting with curses and ironically prayed that God might help him. At these words of bitterness and malice the man of God flushed deeply, for he now realized that they had come to work him injury. Whereupon fitz Urse, who seemed to be their leader and more prepared for the crime than the others, breathing fury, broke out in these words: "We have somewhat to say to thee by the king's command; say if thou wilt that we tell it here before all." But the archbishop knew what they were about to say and answered, "These things should not be spoken in private or in the chamber, but in public." Now these wretches so burned for the slaughter of the archbishop that if the door-keeper had not called back the clerks—for the archbishop had ordered them all to withdraw—they would have killed him with the shaft of his cross which stood by as they afterwards confessed. When those who had gone out returned, he, who had before reviled the archbishop, again addressed him saying, "When the king made peace with you and all disputes were settled, he sent you back to your own

see, as you requested; but you, in contrary fashion, adding insult
to injury, have broken the peace, and in your pride have wrought
evil in yourself against your lord. For, those by whose ministry
the king's son was crowned and invested with the honours of
sovereignty, you with obstinate pride have condemned with
sentence of suspension. You have also bound with the chain of
anathema those servants of the king by whose counsel and prudence the business of the kingdom is transacted. From this it is
manifest that you would take away the crown from the king's
son if you had the power. But now the plots and schemes you
have hatched in order to carry out your designs against your
lord the king are known to all men. Say therefore whether you
are prepared to come into the king's presence and make answer
to these charges." The archbishop replied, "Never was it my wish,
as God is my witness, to take away the crown from my lord the
king's son or to diminish his power; rather would I wish him
three crowns and help him to obtain the greatest realms of the
earth, so it be with right and equity. But it is unjust that my
lord the king should be offended because my people accompany
me through the towns and cities and come out to meet me, when
for seven years now they have been deprived through my exile
of the consolation of my presence. Even now I am ready to
satisfy my lord wherever he pleases, if in anything I have done
amiss; but he has forbidden me with threats to enter any of his
cities and towns, or even villages. Moreover, it was not by me,
but by the lord pope that the prelates were suspended from
office." "It was through you," said the infuriated knights, "that
they were suspended; do you absolve them?" "I do not deny," he
answered, "that it was done through me, but it is beyond my
power and utterly incompatible with my dignity to absolve those
whom the lord pope has bound. Let them go to him, on whom
redounds the injury and contempt they have shown towards me
and their mother, the Church of Christ at Canterbury."

"Well then," said these butchers, "this is the king's command,
that you depart with all your men from the kingdom and the
lands which own his dominion; for from this day forth there
can be no peace betwixt him and you or any of yours, for you
have broken the peace." To this the archbishop answered, "Cease
your threats and still your brawling. I put my trust in the king

of Heaven who for his own suffered on the Cross; for from this day forth no one shall see the sea between me and my church. I have not come back to flee again; here shall he who wants me find me. It is not fitting for the king to issue such commands; sufficient are the insults received by me and mine from the king's servants, without further threats." "Such were the king's commands," they replied, "and we will make them good, for whereas you ought to have shown respect to the king's majesty and submitted your vengeance to his judgment, you have followed the impulse of your passion and basely thrust out from the Church his ministers and servants." At these words Christ's champion, rising in fervour of spirit against his accusers, exclaimed, "Whoever shall presume to violate the decrees of the holy Roman see or the laws of Christ's Church, and shall refuse to come of his own accord and make satisfaction, whosoever he be, I will not spare him, nor will I delay to inflict ecclesiastical censures upon the delinquent."

Confounded by these words, the knights sprang to their feet, for they could no longer bear the firmness of his answers. Coming close up to him they said, "We declare to you that you have spoken in peril of your head." Are you then come to slay me?" said he. "I have committed my cause to the great Judge of all mankind; wherefore I am not moved by threats, nor are your swords more ready to strike than is my soul for martyrdom. Go, seek him who would fly from you; me you will find foot to foot in the battle of the Lord." As they retired amidst tumult and insults, he who was fitly surnamed "the bear" brutishly cried out, "In the king's name we command you, both clerks and monks, to seize and hold that man, lest he escape by flight ere the king take full justice on his body." As they departed with these words the man of God followed them to the door and cried out after them, "Here, here will you find me"; putting his hand on his neck, as though marking beforehand the place where they were to strike.

The archbishop then returned to the place where he had before been seated, consoled his clerks and exhorted them not to fear; and, so it seemed to us who were present, he sat there waiting as unperturbed, although his death alone was sought, as if they had come to invite him to a wedding. Ere long back came the mur-

derers in full armour, with swords, axes and hatchets, and other
implements suitable for the crime on which their minds were
set. Finding the doors barred and unopened at their knocking,
they turned aside by a private path through an orchard till they
came to a wooden partition, which they cut and hacked and
finally broke down. Terrified by the noise and uproar, almost all
the clerks and the servants were scattered hither and thither like
sheep before wolves. Those who remained cried out to the archbishop to flee to the church; but he, mindful of his former promise that he would not through fear of death flee from those who
kill the body, rejected flight. For in such case it were not meet to
flee from city to city, but rather to set an example to those subject
to him, so that every one of them should choose to die by the
sword rather than see the divine law set at naught and the sacred
canons subverted. Moreover, he who had long since yearned for
martyrdom, now saw that the occasion to embrace it had seem-
ingly arrived, and dreaded lest it should be deferred or even altogether lost, if he took refuge in the church. But the monks still
pressed him, saying that it was not becoming for him to absent
himself from vespers, which were at that very moment being
said in the church. He lingered for a while motionless in that
less sacred spot, deliberately awaiting that happy hour of con-
summation which he had craved with many sighs and sought
with such devotion; for he feared lest, as has been said, reverence
for the sanctity of the sacred building might deter even the impious from their purpose and cheat him of his heart's desire. For
being confident that after martyrdom he would pass from his
vale of misery, he is reported to have said in the hearing of many
after his return from exile, "You have here a martyr, Alphege,
beloved of God and a true saint; the divine compassion will provide you with yet another; he will not tarry." O pure and trust-
ful was the conscience of that good shepherd, who in defending
the cause of his flock would not delay the hour of his own death,
when it was in his power to do so, nor shun the executioner,
that the fury of the wolves, satiated with the blood of the shepherd, might spare the sheep. But when he would not be persuaded
by argument or entreaties to take refuge in the church, the monks
seized hold of him in spite of his resistance, and pulled, dragged
and pushed him; without heeding his opposition and his clamour

to let him go, they brought him as far as the church. But the door, which led to the monks' cloister, had been carefully barred several days before, and as the murderers were already pressing on their heels, all hope of escape seemed removed. But one of them, running forward, seized hold of the bolt, and to the great surprise of them all, drew it out with as much ease as if it had been merely glued to the door.

After the monks had retreated within the precincts of the church, the four knights came following hard on their heels with rapid strides. They were accompanied by a certain subdeacon called Hugh, armed with malice like their own, appropriately named Mauclerc, being one who showed no reverence either to God or his saints, he he proved by his subsequent action. As soon as the archbishop entered the monastic buildings, the monks ceased the vespers, which they had already begun to offer to God, and ran to meet him, glorifying God for that they saw their father alive and unharmed, when they had heard he was dead. They also hastened to ward off the foe from the slaughter of their shepherd by fastening the bolts of the folding doors giving access the church. But Christ's doughty champion turned to them and ordered the doors to be thrown open, saying, "It is not meant to make a fortress of the house of prayer, the Church of Christ, which, even if it be not closed affords sufficient protection to its children; by suffering rather than by fighting shall we triumph over the enemy; for we are come to suffer, not to resist." Straightway these sacrilegious men, with drawn swords, entered the house of peace and reconciliation, causing no little horror to those present by the mere sight of them and the clash of their armour. All the onlookers were in tumult and consternation, for by this time who had been singing vespers had rushed up to the scene of death.

In a spirit of mad fury the knights called out, "Where is Thomas Becket, traitor to the king and the realm?" When he returned no answer, they cried out the more loudly and insistently, "Where is the archbishop?" At this quite undaunted, as it is written, "The righteous shall be bold as a lion and without fear," he descended from the steps, whither he had been dragged by the monks through their fear of the knights, and in a perfectly clear voice answered, "Lo! here am I, no traitor to the

king, but a priest. What do you seek from me? And whereas he
had already told them that he had no fear of them, he now added,
"Behold, I am ready to suffer in His Name who redeemed me by
His Blood. Far be it from me to flee from your swords, or to
depart from righteousness." Having thus said, he turned aside to
the right, under a pillar, having on one side the altar of the blessed
Mother of God, Mary ever-Virgin, on the other, that of the holy
confessor, Benedict, by whose example and prayers, having cru-
cified the world and its lusts, he endured whatsoever the murderers did to him with such constancy of soul, as if he were no
longer in the flesh. The murderers pursued him. "Absolve," they
cried, "and restore to communion those whom you have excommunicated, and the functions of their office to the others who
have been suspended." He answered, "There has been no satisfaction made, and I will not absolve them." "Then you shall die
this instant," they cried, "and receive your desert." "I, too," said
he, "am ready to die for my Lord, that in my blood the Church
may obtain peace and liberty; but in the name of Almighty God
I forbid you to harm any of my men, whether clerk or lay."
Thus did the noble martyr provide piously for his followers, and
prudently for himself, in that no one standing near should be
hurt nor the innocent oppressed, lest any serious mishap befalling
any that stood by him should dim the lustre of his glory as his
soul sped up to Christ. Most fitting was it that the soldier-martyr
should follow in the footsteps of his Captain and Saviour, who,
when the wicked sought to take him, said, "If ye seek me, let
these go their way."

Then they made a rush at him and laid sacrilegious hands upon
him, pulling and dragging him roughly and violently, endeavouring to get him outside the walls of the church and there slay
him and carry him off prisoner, as they afterwards confessed
was their intention. But as he could not easily be moved from
the pillar, one of them seized hold of him and clung to him more
closely. The archbishop shook him off vigorously, calling him a
pandar and saying, "Touch me not, Reginald; you owe me fealty
and obedience; you are acting like a madman, you and your ac-
complices." All aflame with a terrible fury at this rebuff, the
knight brandished his sword against that consecrated head.
"Neither faith," he cried, "nor obedience do I owe you against

my fealty to my lord the king." Then the unconquered martyr understood that the hour was approaching that should release him from the miseries of this mortal life, and that the crown of immortality prepared for him and promised by the Lord was already nigh at hand. Whereupon, inclining his head as one in prayer and joining his hands together and uplifting them, he commended his cause and that of the Church of God and St. Mary and the blessed martyr, St. Denys. Scarce had he uttered the words than the wicked knight, fearing lest he should be rescued by the people and escape alive, leapt suddenly upon him and wounded the sacrificial lamb of God in the head, cutting off the top of the crown which the unction of the sacred chrism had dedicated to God, and by the same stroke he almost cut off the arm of him who tells the story. For he, when all the others, both monks and clerks had fled, steadfastly stood by the saintly archbishop and held his arms around him, till the one he opposed to the blow was almost severed. Behold the simplicity of the dove, the wisdom of the serpent in this martyr who presented his body to the strikers that he might preserve his head, that is to say, his soul and the Church, unharmed, nor would he take any forethought or employ any stratagem against those who slay the body whereby he might escape. O worthy shepherd, who gave himself so boldly to the wolves, in order that his flock might not be torn to pieces! Because he had cast away the world, the world in seeking to crush him unconsciously exalted him.

Next he received a second blow on the head, but still he stood firm and immovable. At the third blow he fell on his knees and elbows, offering himself a living sacrifice and saying in a low voice, "For the Name of Jesus and the protection of the Church I am ready to embrace death." But the third knight inflicted a terrible wound as he lay prostrate. By this stroke the sword was dashed against the pavement and the crown of his head, which was large, was separated from the head in such a way that the blood white with the brain and the brain no less red from the blood, dyed the floor of the cathedral with the white of the lily and the red of the rose, the colours of the Virgin and Mother and of the life and death of the martyr and confessor. The fourth knight warded off any who sought to intervene, so that the others might with greater freedom and licence perpetrate the crime. But the fifth—no knight he, but that same clerk who had entered with the knights—that a fifth blow might not be wanting to the martyr in who other things had imitated Christ, placed his foot on the neck of the holy priest and precious martyr and, horrible to relate, scattered the brains and blood about the pavement, crying out to the others, "Let us away, knights, this fellow will rise no more."

In all his sufferings the illustrious martyr displayed an incredible steadfastness. Neither with hand nor robe, as is the manner of human frailty, did he oppose the fatal stroke. Nor when smitten did he utter a single word, neither cry nor groan, nor any sound indicative of pain. But he held motionless the head which he had bent to meet the uplifted sword until, bespattered with blood and brains, as though in an attitude of prayer, his body lay prone on the pavement, while his soul rested in Abraham's bosom.

PART TWO

Eighteenth Century Views

EIGHTEENTH CENTURY VIEWS
INTRODUCTION

From the eighteenth century we find an unusually clear exchange of statements for and against Becket. Lord Lyttelton, whose scholarship represents the aggressive kind of rationalism that often characterized the so-called enlightenment, wrote a massive three-volume biography of Henry II. His sympathies are clear from the two brief selections from it that follow. Becket was guilty of "evasive reserve" and "wilful and premeditated prejury," he was "excessively passionate, haughty, and vainglorious," and he acted "from motives of arrogance and ambition."

While Lord Lyttelton spoke for the anticlerical element among his literate contemporaries, it was inevitable that a spokesman for the traditional position of the church should reply with equal passion. The Reverend Joseph Berington undertook the task, and in a volume not nearly as long or as thorough as Lord Lyttelton's he implies that the latter falsified the case "from the prejudications of low bigotry, from dislike of characters, or from a paltry policy." As for Becket, even in retreat he was doing "what every honest man should have done," while Henry, "like a tyrant from the east," sought "to gratify revenge, and to triumph in the humiliation of a man, who had dared to oppose him."

These two selections contain classical summations of the opposing views. They also provide glimpses of eighteenth century historical writing by two men who obviously cared deeply about their subject. Each writer chose a different hero to defend, and each found a substantially different way to interpret what happened at Clarendon in 1164.

10   *George Lord Lyttelton*
                         Henry the Second

One of the means, by which Becket, in concert with Alexander, judged, that the schemes they had formed together might best be promoted, was the canonization of archbishop Anselm. The cause, which they both equally determined to maintain, was the very same which that prelate had eminently distinguished himself in supporting, and for which he had suffered banishment, with many other evils, under two kings of England. To canonize him was to sanctify that cause and those sufferings: it was crowning opposition to the laws of the English government with the glory of heaven: nor could there be found a more proper or a more powerful artifice to seduce the imagination of the ignorant vulgar, and prevail with them to second the zeal of Becket in a future contest with the crown. For this purpose the archbishop had before employed John of Salisbury to compile a book, chiefly drawn from the writings of Eadmer, a monk contemporary with Anselm, in which, with an account of the merit of that prelate to the see of Rome and the church, several miracles, said to have been done by him during his life, and after his death, were recorded. This was presented to Alexander in the council, as a sufficient foundation for inserting him in the catalogue of saints. But that pontiff, though his own inclinations corresponded with this request, was afraid to grant it at this time, because the same honor was asked for many other persons; and therefore he waited till after the council was separated, and sent into England a bull, by which Becket was impowered to convene his suffragan bishops, together with the clergy of his province, and, in case that they should approve of it, to canonize Anselm. Nevertheless, it seems that the archbishop, upon the breaking out of the quarrel between him and the king, was afraid of irritating him more by

SOURCE. George Lord Lyttelton, *The History of the Life of King Henry the Second and of the Age in Which He Lived,* Vol. II, Dublin: Printed by and for George Faulkner, MDCCLXVIII, pp. 373–377, 644–645.

an act of this nature, or was doubtful whether his suffragans would concur with him in it: for we do not find that he assembled any synod upon it; and the canonization of Anselm was deferred for several centuries, even till the reign of King Henry the Seventh. But other parts of the plan concerted with Alexander were prosecuted by Becket, upon his return into England, with all the violence natural to his vehement temper. A severe canon having been made in the council of Tours against any persons who usurped the goods of the church, he took occasion from thence to set up several claims, as archbishop of Canterbury, to the lands of English barons. Particularly he demanded of Roger de Clare, earl of Hertford, the castle of Tunbridge, with the honor belonging thereunto, though it had been granted in exchange for the castle of Brione in Normandy to the great grandfather of the earl, by King William the First, and quietly enjoyed, from that time, by the grantee and his heirs, under homage to the crown; alledging, that it had formerly belonged to his see, and that no grant, nor any length of possession, could be good against the claim of the church, according to the maxims of the Roman canon law. This alarmed all the nobility, who knew not how far his resumptions might be carried. The king himself was not safe with respect to his own property: for certain castles and manors of the royal demesne were claimed by the archbishop, as alienations from the see of Canterbury, the restitution of which he was in conscience obliged to procure. It would be tedious to enumerate each particular instance, wherein, by a real or pretended zeal for the church, he disquieted his fellow-subjects, or offended his sovereign, but it is necessary to take notice of one, which was of a nature somewhat different from the others, and very material. He collated a priest, named Lawrence, to the rectory of Eynesford in Kent, against the right of patronage in the lord of the manor, William de Eynesford, who held of the archbishoprick, but was also an immediate tenant of the king. The pretence on which this was done was a general prerogative, which Becket supposed inherent in the archbishop of Canterbury, to present to all benefices in the manors of his tenants. As the claim was unprecedented, William drove out the servants who were sent by Lawrence to take possession of the church in his name. Becket did not condescend to determine the dispute by process

of law, but excommunicated his adversary, and without having
asked the king's consent. This was a direct attack on the royal
prerogatives. For it had been an uncontroverted right of the
crown ever since the establishment of the feudal constitution by
William the First, that neither the tenants in chief, nor the servants of the king, could be excommunicated without his knowledge and consent, because the consequences of that sentence
would deprive him of their service. But Becket, who disregarded
both the authority and the reason of all such laws as tended to
restrain or controul the ecclesiastical power, answered Henry,
who sent him an order to take off the excommunication, that
it did not belong to him to command any person to be excommunicated or absolved. Nevertheless, when he found that the
king insisted upon it, he yielded at last: but it does not appear,
that he made any excuse for what he had done, or acknowledged
the right of patronage in the lord of the manor, or receded in the
least from the principles on which he had acted.

All these proceedings, instead of intimidating Henry, or avert-
ing him, by the prospect of a violent opposition, from his intention of reducing the clery to obedience, determined him to it
more strongly. He saw, indeed, that he must expect to find in
Becket, whose assistance he had hoped for, his most intractable
adversary; but he saw likewise, that this circumstance, however
unfortunate, rendered it necessary to proceed with double vigour,
in order to set timely bounds to the insolence of a prelate, who,
if he was suffered any longer to go on uncontrouled, would give
such spirit and strength to the ecclesiastical faction, that it would
not be afterwards in the power of the crown to vindicate its
own dignity, and the right of the kingdom. He thought that the
first beginning of the reformation he meditated would be most
properly made, by taking from the clergy that strange privilege,
to which they pretended, of being exempt from all secular judi-
cature; because, so long as they retained it, they might safely per-
severe in all their other encroachments on the civil authority. And
he had now on occasion of bringing on the question, with the
strongest evidences of the mischiefs that must attend the con-
tinuance of such an immunity. Becket had lately protected some
clergymen, guilty of enormous and capital crimes, from being
delivered up to the justice of the crown. Among others there

was one accused of having debauched a gentleman's daughter, and of having, to secure his enjoyment of her, murdered the father. The king required him to be brought to judgment before a civil tribunal, that, if convicted, he might suffer a penalty adequate to his guilt, which the ecclesiastical judicatures could not inflict upon him: but this was resisted by Becket; which raising a general indignation in the publick, Henry summoned all the bishops to attend him at Westminster, and declared to them, in a weighty and vehement speech, the reasons of their meeting. He began by complaining of the flagrant corruption of the spiritual courts, which, in many cases, extorted great sums from the innocent, and in others allowed the guilty to escape with no punishment, but pecuniary commutations, which turned to the profit of the clergy. By these methods, he said, they had levied in a year more money from the people than he did himself, but left wickedness unreformed, secure, and triumphant. He then set forth to them, in strong colours, the very great mischiefs that the whole kingdom had suffered, and the yet greater that necessarily must be expected to arise, from the impunity of the most flagitous offenders, who, under the cover of holy orders, had nothing to apprehend except spiritual censures, which wicked men little regarded. He said, it was certain, that they would only be readier to offend than before, if, after the spiritual punishment, they were not liable to corporal pains: and observed, that, on account of the abuse of their holy character, they deserved to be treated with more severity than any other delinquents. For these reasons he demanded the consent of the bishops, that ecclesiasticks convicted, or confessing themselves guilty, of any heinous crime, should first be degraded, and then immediately delivered over to the secular courts, for corporal punishment: he also desired, that one of his officers might always be present at the degradation of any such offenders, to prevent their flying from justice.

Becket was conscious that these complaints, though they seemed to be general, had a particular reference to some of his late proceedings. He likewise knew that all the laity, and even many of the clergy, had been displeased at his conduct: nor could he be sure that the demands which Henry had made, on such a foundation of justice, and with so much moderation, would not be agreed to by the bishops, if they were to give him an imme-

diate answer, while the impression of his speech was strong on
their minds. He therefore laboured very earnestly to obtain his
consent, that no opinion should be delivered by them upon what
he had said, till the next morning. This was denied; but he was
suffered to confer with them apart; and, though he found them
inclined to yield to a proposition, supported, not only by reason
and the law of the land, but (as most of them acknowledged)
by the scripture itself, yet he so wrought upon them by arguments drawn from the canons, the authority of which had entirely taken place of the scripture, that, coming over to his opinion, they unanimously joined with him in declaring to the king,
that no ecclesiastick ought ever to be judged in a secular court,
or suffer death, or loss of limb, for any crime whatsoever; and
that, degradation from orders being a punishment, it would be
unjust to punish twice for the same crime: but that, if a clergyman, who had been degraded, should afterwards be guilty of
other crimes, the royal judges, in that case, might punish him for
them, according to their discretion.

. . . Thus in the fifty-third year of his age, was assassinated
Thomas Becket; a man of great talents, of elevated thoughts, and
of invincible courage; but of a most violent and turbulent spirit;
excessively passionate, haughty, and vainglorious; in his resolu-
tions inflexible, in his resentment implacable. It cannot be denied
that he was guilty of a wilful and premeditated perjury: that he
opposed the necessary course of publick justice, and acted in
defiance of the laws of his country; laws which he had most
solemnly acknowledged and confirmed: nor is it less evident,
that, during the heat of this dispute, he was in the highest degree
ungrateful to a very kind master, whose confidence in him had
been boundless, and who from a private condition had advanced
him to be the second man in his kingdom. On what motives he
acted can certainly be judged of by Him alone, to whom all hearts
are open. He might be misled by the prejudices of a bigotted age,
and think he was doing an acceptable service to God, in con-
tending, even to death, for the utmost excess of ecclesiastical
and papal authority. Yet the strength of his understanding, his
conversation in courts and camps, among persons whose notions
were more free and enlarged, the different colour of his former
life, and the suddenness of the change which seemed to be wrought

in him upon his election to Canterbury, would make one suspect, as many did in the times wherein he lived, that he only became the champion of the church from an ambitious desire of sharing its power; a power more independent of the favor of the king, and therefore more agreeable to the haughtiness of his mind, than that which he had enjoyed as a minister of the crown. And this suspicion is encreased by the marks of cunning and falseness, which are evidently seen in his conduct on some occasions. Neither is it impossible, that, when first he assumed his new character, he might act the part of a zealot, merely or principally from motives of arrogance and ambition; yet, afterwards, being engaged, and inflawed by the contest, work himself up into a real enthusiasm. The continual praises of those with whom he acted, the honors done him in his exile by all the clergy of France, and the vanity which appears so predominant in his mind, may have conduced to operate such a change. He certainly shewed in the latter part of his life a spirit as fervent as the warmest enthusiast's; such a spirit indeed as constitutes heriosm, when it exerts itself in a cause beneficial to mankind. Had he defended the established laws of his country, and the fundamental rules of civil justice, with as much zeal and intrepidity as he opposed them, he would have deserved to be ranked with those great men, whose virtues make one easily forget the allay of some natural imperfections: but, unhappily, his good qualities were so misapplied, that they became no less hurtful to the public weal of the kingdom, than the worst of his vices.

11 *Joseph Berington*
Henry the Second

Men, whom nature has not formed in common moulds, whose understandings are large, and whose hearts swell, can only be engaged by objects commensurate with their capacities. When

SOURCE. The Rev. Joseph Berington, *The History of the Reign of Henry the Second, and of Richard and John, His Sons,* London: G. G. J. & J. Robinson, R. Faulder, 1790, pp. 62–63, 72–78.

Becket was the minister of a monarch, whose empire was extensive, and whose views were vast, the situation harmonized with his character, and he could be munificent, and ostentatious, and soldier-like as he. Nor can we wonder, if the looser manners of the age, and the occupations of the busy scene, should have more than reconciled him to employments, which seem not to have become the clergyman. There were examples in the French court, and more in that of Frederick. Besides, Theobald had himself raised him to the station, who knew its offices and all its calls. But when the primacy of England was in his hands, with its splendid honours and its thousand duties, the charge alone was amply sufficient; and it could occupy and engross his thoughts. His manners and his views would naturally bend to it; and that cast of character which had fortunately carried him to the objects of his ambition, would now operate to similar exertions in his new department. Now also, he might think, he was become the servant of a greater potentate, than was Henry Plantaganet, namely, of Alexander, the Roman pontiff. It was the prejudice of the age. And may it not be said, that religion and a sense of duty did likewise co-operate to the reformation of manners and the change of character, of which I am speaking? New features of mind, and a sternness of virtue might be then produced, of which before no symptoms had been exhibited. The mind of man is a system of effects. To say then, that the archbishop was insincere in his conversion, and affected new manners, from sinister and insidious views, is ungenerous and contrary to the declarations of the most contemporary writers; but not to be able to see that the transition was most natural, as agreeable to the ordinary phenomena of human nature, speaks a want of discernment, of which who is vacant, should not attempt to relate events in which *man* is a principal agent; and to be conscious of truth, and to misstate it, from the prejudications of low bigotry, from dislike of characters, or from paltry policy, is of prejudice the basest species, and degrades the historian.

. . . The report of the quarrel between Henry and his prelates excited general attention, and as interest, or better motives preponderated, so men judged. Alexander would naturally applaud the firmness of the bishops; but as his obligations to the king were manifold, and he still wanted all his aid, his situation became peculiarly delicate.—The bishop of Lisieux, about this time, came to England. He found the nation divided into parties, the king violently agitated, and many of the episcopal order in great consternation. The primate only bore his head aloft, and braved the storm. The wily Norman, who well saw he must espouse some party, was preplexed. To incur the anger of his master he was not disposed; and he was aware how warm upon the recollection of the bishops must be the harangue, on the liberties of the church, which he had pronounced at Tours. Strenuously did he labour to restore peace; but in vain. He then advised the king, if possible, to divide the bishops, that their power might be weakened. The advice was neither generous nor honourable; but it succeeded. Roger of York was persuaded to desert the confederacy, and he was soon followed by others, who now enforced the propriety of the king's demand, and vehemently solicited the primate to resist no longer. The king, they said, had all power in his hands, and was inflexibly determined; and would he, for the sake of a single expression, expose himself and the church to dangers, which his submission could only avert?

Other means were also employed, promises, caresses, entreaties. Noblemen of the first distinction, in the monarch's name, waited on him. They pressed him by every argument, such as the bishops had used; and they added others. They mentioned his obligations to the king; the evils which had already followed their disunion; and they talked of the folly of hazarding all for a trifle. It seems as if England and all the foreign provinces were at stake!

. . . Three months elapsed, before the bishops with their primate were again summoned to appear. It is not related, why the king was so dilatory in bringing a question to issue in which he seemed to be much interested; which was to fix a bar, modern writers tell us, against clerical encroachments; and when the haughty Becket, with his adherents, would be humbled at his feet. As the business was important, we may fairly presume, that leisure was required to digest its several parts. The wise heads of the nation must be consulted, that each royal and ancient custom be exactly defined, and be ready to be produced, with such evidence of authenticity, that cavil and opposition shall at once be silenced. In the confusion, which the troubles of the civil war had introduced, and more than that, in the collision of Saxon and

Norman laws and usages, it must be no easy task to ascertain, with precision, even the limits of the civil power, much less to determine the exact boundaries of the two rival jurisdictions. The day at last was fixed, and a general council of the nation was summoned to Clarendon, a royal palace near Salisbury, for the 28th of January, 1164.

They met, all the prelates, abbots, priors, earls, barons and great men of the land. John of Oxford, one of the king's chaplains, presided; and Henry took his seat.—Abruptly, then, it seems, he called on the bishops to perform their promise, and with threats urged them to submit. The primate who, from the beginning, had suspected the king's intentions, was alarmed by this intemperate exordium, and expressed a design (proposuit)[1] of receding from the imprudent engagement, he had, in a manner, been compelled to make. At this, Henry's rage was extreme: in the eyes of the council it bore the appearance of a phrensy. He menaced banishment and death. Those bishops who, as yet, had not deserted the primate, were stricken as by a thunderbolt. They crowded round him, and with tears entreat that he will relent, as his person, the safety of the clergy, and their own lives were at stake. . . . The strong remonstrance, thus pathetically expressed, had its effect. It seemed to intimate that the drawn dagger was even now pointed at his heart. Indeed, some of the king's guards were running through the chambers with naked swords, their garments tucked up, and ready for execution.—Struggling with his own resolution, yet affected for the sake of others, the primate now signified that he would obey the king's will; and then promised that, "on the word of truth, he would observe the ancient customs of the realm." The bishops made the same solemn promise. Forthwith it was proposed, that the customs be recited, and be reduced to order. But now it appeared, "that as yet it was not known, which they were." The urgency of the demand only had excited suspicion. Such of the assembly, therefore, as, from age and experience, might be thought to know them best, were ordered, from memory, to collect them. They had formed a list, and were proceeding to others, when the archbishop observed: "I am not among the elders of the realm, so as

---

[1] From the Latin *proponere*, to put forth; hence, a proposal.

to know what these customs are, nor have I been long in my present office. The matter is weighty, and the day is fast declining; let the further prosecution of the business be made over to the morning." The motion was accepted, and the council rose.

Such, as contemporary historians have recorded, whom I have faithfully copied, were the first day's transactions at Clarendon. On their violence and general treachery the reader will make his own reflections. I only wish to suggest that, as to Becket; when he proposed to recoil from his imprudent engagement; at the imprudent mandate of the king, it was what every honest man should have done. He saw there was no honour in his views. Again, indeed, he gave way, and I will call it a weakness; but what, in like circumstances, would have been the conduct of the most resolved patriot? Promises so extorted are not binding, if, on a cool revision, they displease. I do not say, it was fear absolutely which prevailed the archbishop; but it was a mode of entreaty, as irresistible as it.—As to the members of the meeting, the primate alone excepted, there was not a spark of liberty in their breasts.—As to Henry; he came to Clarendon like a tyrant from the east. It was not to strengthen the arm of justice, to invigorate the laws, to protect the rights of the crown, that he would enforce his royal customs, or he would have come prepared to exhibit them; but to gratify revenge, and to triumph in the humiliation of a man, who had dared to oppose him. It appeared also in his intemperate rage. Henry, I own, in many regards, was a great prince, great in peace and war, and I shall have occasion to show it; but his greatness never once appears in this controversy with Becket.

PART THREE

Nineteenth Century Views

NINETEENTH CENTURY VIEWS
INTRODUCTION

Two forces helped give direction to historical scholarship during the nineteenth century. Increased respect for science and the scientific method was one such force; the second was nationalism. Historians undertook the massive job of gathering, editing, and making available to libraries and to the whole community of scholarship quantities of source material, much of it from the middle ages. National histories on a grand scale began to appear, especially in England and France.

Out of this effort came the nearly two hundred volumes collectively titled *Chronicles and Memorials of Great Britain and Ireland*, popularly called "The Rolls Series" because they were published under the supervision of Great Britain's Master of the Rolls. This series includes seven volumes edited by J. C. Robertson and J. B. Sheppard under the title *Materials for the History of Thomas Becket, Archbishop of Canterbury*. All the contemporary biographies of the saint, including the one by Edward Grim, a portion of which is quoted above, appear in the original Latin in these volumes along with letters, documents, and other source materials.

Robertson, one of the editors, also wrote his own biography of Thomas Becket. His conclusions, based upon long, conscientious study, represent one approach to the historic controversy. Bishop William Stubbs, who edited eleven volumes of the Rolls Series, several dealing with the time of Henry II, is another writer whose work is included in this section.

The professional historian, paid to teach or to write, is a relatively new species, produced largely by the universities of this century. Historians of earlier ages often relied on other sources of livelihood, with the writing of history an avocation and labor of love, though sometimes a profitable labor. Of the five writers selected here to represent the nineteenth century, three were clergymen and two were professional lawyers. These selections obviously do not exhaust the range of viewpoints held in that century. They simply introduce a variety of interpretations and they suggest some elements of the controversy not discussed elsewhere. They reflect the range of Victorian attitudes toward monarchy, the church, and the evolution of common law.

12   *Henry Hart Milman*
      History of Latin Christianity

Henry Hart Milman was a clergyman of the early nineteenth century (1791–1869) with an intriguingly varied range of accomplishments. Modestly successful as a playwright, poet, classicist (he translated for publication the Agamemnon *of Aeschylus and the* Bacchae *of Euripides), writer of hymns, and controversial theologian, he is best remembered by students of history because he edited a reprint of Gibbon's* Decline and Fall of the Roman Empire. *His frequent footnotes in this edition attempt to compensate for Gibbon's anti-Christian rationalism, and they provide a clue to the viewpoint we might expect him to hold regarding a church-state conflict.*

Milman's History of Latin Christianity, *first published in 1855 as a sequel to his earlier* History of Christianity to the Abolition of Paganism in the Roman Empire, *portrays Thomas Becket as an unflinching hero in the face of royal aggression.*

The selection that follows, starting with the arrival of the assassins at Canterbury, indicates the subjective passion of his writing; unlike some of his contemporaries Milman rejects objectivity as the historian's proper goal. In the next selection Robertson quotes Milman's opinion of Henry II in a manner that confirms the point of view that this portion of Milman's writing would suggest.

SOURCE. Henry Hart Milman, *History of Latin Christianity*, Vol. IV, New York: Sheldon and Co., 1860, pp. 414–418.

His friends had more fear for Becket for than Becket himself. The gates were closed and barred, but presently sounds were heard of those without, striving to break in. The lawless Randulph de Broc was hewing at the door with an axe. All around Becket was the confusion of terror: he only was calm. Again spoke John of Salisbury with his cold prudence—"Thou wilt never take counsel: they seek thy life." "I am prepared to die." "We who are sinners are not so weary of life." "God's will be done." The sounds without grew wilder. All around him entreated Becket to seek sanctuary in the church. He refused, whether from religious reluctance that the holy place should be stained with his blood, or from the nobler motive of sparing his assassins this deep aggravation of their crime. They urged that the bell was already tolling for vespers. He seemed to give a reluctant consent; but he would not move without the dignity of his crosier carried before him. With gentle compulsion they half drew, half carried him through a private chamber, they in all the hasty agony of terror, he striving to maintain his solemn state, into the church. The din of the armed men was ringing in the cloister. The affrighted monks broke off the service; some hastened to close the doors; Becket commanded them to desist—"No one should be debarred from entering the house of God." John of Salisbury and the rest fled and hid themselves behind the altars and in other dark places. The Archbishop might have escaped into the dark and intricate crypt, or into the chapel in the roof. There remained only the Canon Robert (of Merton), Fitz-Stephen, and the faithful Edward Grim. Becket stood between the altar of St. Benedict and that of the Virgin. It was thought that Becket contemplated taking his seat on his archiepiscopal throne near the high altar.

Through the open door of the cloister came rushing in the four, fully armed, some with axes in their hands, with two or three wild followers, through the dim and bewildering twilight. The knights shouted aloud, "Where is the traitor?" No answer came back. "Where is the Archbishop?" "Behold me, no traitor, but a priest of God!" Another fierce and rapid altercation followed: they demanded the absolution of the bishops, his own surrender to the King's justice. They strove to seize him to drag him forth from the Church (even they had awe of the holy place), either to kill him without, or to carry him in bonds to the King. He clung to the pillar. In the struggle he grappled with De Tracy, and with desperate strength dashed him on the pavement. His passion rose; he called Fitz-Urse by a foul name, a pander. These were almost his last words (how unlike those of Stephen and the greater than Stephen!) He taunted Fitz-Urse with his fealty sworn to himself. "I owe no fealty but to my King!" returned the maddened soldier, and struck the first blow. Edward Grim interposed his arm, which was almost severed off. The sword struck Becket, but slightly, on the head. Becket received it in an attitude of prayer—"Lord, receive my spirit," with an ejaculation to the Saints of the Church. Blow followed blow (Tracy seems to have dealt the first mortal wound), till all, unless perhaps De Moreville, had wrecked their vengeance. The last, that of Richard de Brito, smote off a piece of his skull. Hugh of Horsea, their follower, a renegade priest surnamed Mauclerk, set his heel upon his neck, and crushed out the blood and brains. "Away!" said the ruffian, "it is time that we were gone." They rushed out to plunder the archiepiscopal palace.

The mangled body was left on the pavement; and when his affrighted followers ventured to approach to perform their last offices, an incident ocurred which, however incongruous, is too characteristic to be suppressed. Amid their adoring awe at his courage and constancy, their profound rapture of wonder and delight on discovering not merely that his whole body was swathed in the coarsest sackcloth, but that his lower garments were swarming with vermin. From that moment miracles began. Even the populace had before been divided; voices had been heard among the crowd denying him to be a martyr; he was but the victim of his own obstinacy. The Archbishop of York even after this dared to preach that it was a judgment of God against Becket—that "he perished, like Pharaoh, in his pride." But the torrent swept away at once all this resistance. The Government inhibited the miracles, but faith in miracles scorns obedience to human laws. The Passion of the Martyr Thomas was saddened and glorified every day with new incidents of its atrocity, of his holy firmness, of wonders wrought by his remains.

The horror of Becket's murder ran throughout Christendom. At first, of course, it was attributed to Henry's direct orders.

Universal hatred branded the King of England with a kind of outlawry, a spontaneous excommunication. William of Sens, though the attached friend of Becket, probably does not exaggerate the public sentiment when he describes this deed as surpassing the cruelty of Herod, the perfidy of Julian, the sacrilege of the traitor Judas.

13   *James C. Robertson*
                         Life of Becket

Like Milman, James Craigie Robertson was a prominent clergyman and author of a general work on church history. He contributed enormously to historical scholarship through his work as editor of the Materials for the History of Archbishop Thomas Becket, *which comprise seven volumes of the Rolls Series. He completed the first volume of this undertaking in 1875; the final volume was edited by a collaborator, J. B. Sheppard, in 1883, a year after Robertson's death.*

His Life of Becket *reaches conclusions decidedly different from Milman's. Although he did not consistently follow the adage, his statement that "It is not for one age to make its own principles the rule for judging of persons who belonged to another age" marks him as a disciple of the newer approaches to historical thinking identified with the scientific influence of the mid-nineteenth century. His conclusion that "modern English liberty" emerged from Becket's exertions is frequently echoed by other writers. Robertson discloses his fear that Becket's program might have made England "the most priest-ridden and debased of modern countries" rather than "the freest"; Becket's name revives for him "manifestations of a spirit which would aim at the establishment of priestly tyranny and injustice."*

In Becket's own time, it was disputed whether he ought to be regarded as a martyr. Robert, Bishop of Hereford, the old pro-

SOURCE. James C. Robertson, *Life of Becket,* London: John Murray, 1859, pp. 311–320.

fessor of Paris and Melun, had proposed by anticipation, with
the coolness of a schoolman, the question whether this title would
belong to the Primate if he should meet with death in his contest
with the King. Grim relates that, on the very day after the
murder, "one of our habit and tonsure"—apparently a monk of
Christchurch at Canterbury—denied his claim, on the ground that
his obstinacy had deserved his fate. The Lambeth biographer
reports that some persons regarded his pretence of justice as
merely a covering for pride and vainglory; that they held him
to have been lacking in that charity without which suffering is of
no avail; to have been fond of pomp, haughty, rapacious, violent,
and cruel; that they argued that, as it is not the pain of death
which makes a martyr, so neither is it his cause alone, but that a
good cause must be accompanied by graces of character and
conduct in which Thomas of Canterbury was manifestly defi-
cient. And we are told that half a century later, in defiance both
of Papal canonization and of popular enthusiasm, the same opinions found their defenders in the University of Paris—nay, that
even the salvation of Becket was called in question. Into the
technical inquiry whether the title of martyr were deserved, it is
unnecessary now to enter, but some estimate of his merits will be
here expected by way of conclusion.

It is not for one age to make its own principles the rule for
judging of persons who belonged to another age; and if there be
anything which honourably distinguishes the tone of history in
our time from that which prevailed during the eighteenth century, it is most especially the disposition to make allowance for
men of earlier times whose ideas and circumstances were widely
different from our own. Yet this allowance may be carried too
far, so as to seduce historical writers into a love of paradox, and
to produce a forgetfulness of the bounds which separate right
from wrong. Without denying that the conduct of a personage
in history may have been justified before his own conscience, we
may rightly ask whether it deserves the gratitude of mankind;
and as to his personal justification, we are entitled to ask not only
whether he acted according to the light which he had, but
whether he was careful to obtain—or whether he did not rather
shut out—the best light which was within his reach. How, then,
will Becket bear such an inquiry? Can we acquit him, if we con-

sider that, however much the principles of this generation might have been corrupted by a long course of falsehoods and forgeries —by the pretended Decretals, by the influence of Hildebrand and his school, by the indiscriminating compilations and perverted glosses of the canonists—the Bible was open to him, and the true history of earlier Christian ages was not wholly overlaid?—that the pretentions which he set up in behalf of the clergy were opposed by many of the most learned ecclesiastics? that his ablest and most confidential adviser was often obliged to disapprove of his proceedings, and earnestly represented to him the danger of inflaming his mind by the study of the books on which his pretensions were grounded? If Richard of Canterbury could argue the question of the clerical immunities in the manner which we have seen, is it to be said that the age is to serve as an excuse for the unreasonable and unscriptural views which Becket so zealously maintained on the subject?

The great fortune of Becket's reputation was the manner of his end. "His behaviour in the act of death," says Daniel; "his courage to take it; his passionate committing the cause of the Church, with his soul, to God and His saints—the place, the time, the manner, and all—aggravates the hatred of the deed, and makes compassion and opinion to be on his side." All that was unseemly in his last struggle was washed away by his blood. The continual expressions of apprehension, and vaunts of his readiness to die, in which he had indulged for years—offensive as they were in themselves, and calumnious towards the King—seemed then to acquire a reflected justification, and even to be invested with the character of prophetic foresight. But, in truth, the crime of his murderers must almost be dismissed from our consideration in endeavouring to form an estimate of his merits. We must judge him mainly by his previous acts; and we must confine ourselves strictly to the real facts of the case, since the utter misrepresentations by which the sympathy of his contemporaries was enlisted on his side render their opinion as worthless as that of those in our own time have allowed themselves to be led by it, without the labour or the desire of acquiring materials for a correct and impartial judgment.

If we condemn Becket, it is by no means necessary that we should acquit his royal antagonist. "Henry the Second," says

Dean Milman, "was a sovereign who, with many noble and kingly qualities, lived, more than even most monarchs of his age, in the direct violation of every Christian precept—of justice, humanity, conjugal, fidelity. He was lustful, cruel, treacherous, arbitrary. But throughout this contest there is no remonstrance whatever from Primate or Pope against his disobedience to the laws of God—only to those of the Church." In endeavouring, therefore, to estimate the conduct of the King and the Archbishop towards each other, our view must be confined to those parts of Henry's character which brought him under the denunciations of the hierarchy. And here—even if we admit all that is imputed to him by his opponents—it seems impossible to approve of Becket's dealings with him. The King was deceived in the fancy that he knew the man whom he promoted to the primacy; whereas, on Henry's part, the contest drew forth nothing for which Becket had not been before prepared. If Henry was violent and false, was it for Becket to begin his primacy by giving the lie to all his former life; and not only to be violent, but to set the example of violence? If there were reason to apprehend that the attack on the immunities of criminal clerks might be followed by some attempt to encroach on the real rights of the Church, was the denial of a plainly reasonable claim the best way of establishing a ground for resistance to such aggressions? and was it for a Christian prelate, not only to oppose the King in a reasonable claim, but to render his opposition more offensive by continual displays of that pride with which his enemies loudly reproach him, which alienated many who were friendly towards him, and which even his most zealous admirers hardly venture to gloss over?

If Becket had been disposed to act as a reformer of the English Church, there was abundant opportunity for his exertions. Without requiring from an ecclesiastic of that age that he should have anticipated the work of the sixteenth century, we may see in the excessive abuse of pluralities, by which the Chancellor himself had largely profited, in the practice of keeping bishoprics long vacant in order that the Crown might appropriate the revenues, and in the grossly irregular lives of many among the clergy —evils which loudly called for redress. By impartially attacking these and other disorders, Becket might have assured himself of

the King's cooperation, and might thus have established a footing
for opposition to any really objectionable measures which might
be attempted. But unfortunately both for the Church and for
his own reputation, we can see nothing of impartiality in his
proceedings. If he urged that bishoprics should be filled up, his
motives were suspected, because all his other exertions were on
the side of the hierarchy—stickling for revenues and for patronage,
for castles and for lands, exaltation of the spiritual above the
temporal power, claims that the clergy should be privileged
above the laity by exemption from the tax-gatherer and hangman.
The anger of the King and the nobles was naturally excited
against a prelate who seemed indisposed to admit that the laity,
the secular government, the Crown, or the law had any rights
whatever against the hierarchy. By taking his stand on the assertion of a privilege utterly unfounded, inconsistent with every
principle of civil government, and practically hurtful even to the
class in whose behalf it was claimed, he rendered hopeless all real
reform either in the administration of the Church or in its relations with the State. Yet the man who committed this grievous
error was one from whom, above all other men, an opposite
policy might have been fairly expected. If, on the one side or
the other, the rights of the Church or the State were liable to be
conceived with a narrowness and a partiality suggested by the
position of individuals, to whom could we look with so much
hope of discovering wider and sounder views as to a man who
had passed from the highest secular office under the Crown to
the highest office in the national Church? From such a man,
surely, it might have been expected that he would

> "know
> Both spiritual pow'r and civil, what means,
> What severs each—the bounds of either sword."

From Becket, whether he had retained the chancellorship with
his archbishopric or had resigned it, we might have expected that
he would endeavour to direct the combined action of the ecclesiastical and the secular power to the good government of the
English people; that, believing both civil and spiritual government to be "ordained of God," he would have discerned that the

real well-being of both must lie, not in opposition, but in har-
monious co-operation. Such a view was not hidden from the apprehension of his contemporaries, as may be seen by the language
of Rotrou, and by that of the more moderate Imperialists, from
the time of the contest between Hildebrand and Henry the
Fourth. But Becket could only see in the relations of Church and
State an "incurable duality"; to him it seemed that the servant
of the one must be the enemy of the other; and as, when Chancellor, he had lent himself to measures of oppression against the
Church, so, after having become Archbishop, he had no feeling
but for the most exclusive claims of the clergy. Dr. Lingard's
remark that, "by uniting in himself the offices of Chancellor and
Archbishop, he might in all probability have ruled without
control in Church and State," therefore, instead of justifying
Becket, suggests a ground of severe condemnation against him.
For it was not from any want of ambition or from any indifference to power, that the Archbishop resigned the chancellorship,
but because he had been led by a false and narrow theory to believe that Church and State must be irreconcilably hostile to each
other; and thus he thrust from him such opportunities of affecting
good as few men have ever enjoyed, that he might suffer exile
and death for a groundless and mischievous pretension.

If we compare Becket with the two great champions of the
hierarchy who within a century had preceded him—Gregory the
Seventh and Anselm—the result will not be in his favour. He had
nothing of Hildebrand's originality of conception—of his world-
wide view—of his superiority to vulgar objects —of his far-sighted
patience. Doubtless he would have been ready to adopt the great
Pope's dying words, that he suffered because he had "loved
righteousness, and hated iniquity"; but how much more of self-
deceit would have been necessary for this in the one case than in
the other! Hildebrand, while he exalted the hierarchy against the
secular power, had laboured with an earnest, although partly mis-
directed zeal, that its members should not be unworthy of the
lofty part which he assigned to it in the economy of this world:
in Becket we see the Hildebrandine principles misapplied to shelter the clergy from the temporal punishment of their crimes.
Far less will the later English Primate endure a comparison with
his illustrious predecessor Anselm. It is, indeed, no reproach to

him that he was without that profound philosophical genius which made Anselm the greatest teacher that the Church had seen since St. Augustine; but the deep and mystical fervour of devotion, the calm and gentle temper, the light, keen, and subtle, yet kindly wit, the amiable and unassuming character of Anselm— the absence of all personal pretension in his assertion of the Church's claims—are qualities which fairly enter into the comparison, and which contrast strikingly with the coarse worldly pride and ostentation by which the character and the religion of Becket were disfigured. Nor in a comparison either with Anselm or with Hildebrand must we forget that, while their training had been exclusively clerical and monastic, Becket's more varied experience of life renders the excesses of hierarchical spirit far less excusable in him than in them.

An eminent writer, whose position is very different from that of Becket's ordinary admirers, has eulogised him as having contributed to maintain the balance of moral against physical force, to control the despotism which oppressed the middle ages, and so to prepare the way for modern English liberty. And such was, unquestionably, the result of his exertions, as of much besides in the labours of Hildebrand and his followers. But it is rather an effect wrought out by an over-ruling Providence than anything which Becket contemplated, or for which he deserves credit or gratitude. His efforts were made, not in the general cause of the community, but for the narrowest interests of the clergy as a body separate from other men; and it is not to the freest but to the most priest-ridden and debased of modern countries that we ought to look for the consequences which would have followed, if the course of things had answered to Becket's intention.

Least of all does Becket deserve the sympathy of those among ourselves who dread that reversed Hildebrandism which would reduce the Church to a mere function of the secular power. An Englishman ought no more, as a churchman, to espouse the cause of those who in former times exaggerated the claims of the hierarchy, than, as the subject of a constitutional monarchy, he ought to defend the excesses of despotism. The name of Becket, instead of serving as a safeguard to those who fear encroachment on the Church in our own time, will only furnish their opponents with a pretext for representing the most equitable claims in behalf of the Church as manifestations of a spirit which would aim at the establishment of priestly tyranny and intolerance.

14　　*William Stubbs*
Historical Introductions to the Rolls Series

In the late nineteenth and early twentieth centuries the work of Bishop William Stubbs enjoyed a reputation for scholarship and expertise that was almost beyond dispute, but he has lately become the subject of controversy and challenge. Although he still has his supporters, his opponents have attacked his writing with the fury reserved for a new generation's response to its elders.

For many years Stubbs's three-volume Constitutional History of England *stood as a monumental classic. But the* Constitutional History *is not the real memorial to his scholarly reputation. It was the insight and analysis that he applied to his assignment as editor of various medieval chronicles that led an Oxford colleague to write: "No sounder guide to the times of Henry II, Richard I, John, Edward I, and Edward II has ever been written."[1] Even those who accept that judgment might be reluctant today to share the same writer's opinion that "probably no historian has ever lived who did more for the study of English History than Bishop Stubbs."[2]*

The following excerpt is from Stubb's essay introducing the Rolls Series edition of The Chronicle of the Reigns of Henry II and Richard I. *In the essay the bishop summarizes the basic nature of the problems facing King Henry and then offers his own historical evaluation of the two adversaries, Henry and Becket.*

It is obvious that Henry's great design as well as the subordinate parts of it may, taken apart from the general tenour of his

[1] Arthur Hassell, Preface to *The Historical Introductions to the Rolls Series*, Longmans, Green and Co., London, 1902, p. v.

[2] Ibid., p. vi.

SOURCE. William Stubbs, *Historical Introductions to the Rolls Series*, New York: Longmans, Green and Co., 1902; Crown copyright, pp. 100–103. Reprinted by permission.

character, be read in two ways, or rather that two opposing views of his character may be drawn from the bare consideration of his objects and measures. It may seem that he wished to create a tyranny, to overthrow every vestige of independence among the clergy and nobles, and to provide himself from the proceeds of taxation with means of carrying out personal selfish designs. He might be a man who could endure no opposition, and to whom it was enough to make a thing intolerable that it should be originated by any other than himself. Such a reading would explain much of his avarice, cruelty, and greediness in acquiring territory.

Or it might be argued that as so many of his schemes did actually result in the amelioration of the condition of his subjects, as his judicial reforms were the basis on which the next generation was enabled to raise the earlier stages of civil liberty; and as his ecclesiastical measures have in nearly every particular been sanctioned and adopted by the practice of later ages, he is therefore entitled to the praise of a well-intentioned, benevolent ruler, as well as to the credit of a far-sighted statesman.

Both of these views have been advocated, the first by some of his contemporaries, and those who in later times have approached the history from their point of prejudice; the latter by those who, both anciently and recently, have been inclined to look with too professional an eye on the character of his reforms. I have stated already that I think neither of them tenable; and as it is at present Henry's personal character that is before me, I will give the reasons.

As to the first theory, which, in the mouths of his contemporaries, seems so condemnatory, it must be said that gratuitous baseness was no part of Henry's character, if we may judge by his actions. He was thoroughly unscrupulous and unprincipled, but he was not a tyrant; he was not wantonly cruel or oppressive. His crimes against public law and order, such as they were, were not purposeless, nor is it in any way necessary to suppose that he had that intolerance of all opposition which pursues tyranny for its own sake. He had definite aims, and followed them unrelentingly; whatever could be made to minister to their furtherance was forced to its use. As his passions gave way to his policy, so the minor measures of his policy were sometimes compelled to give way to the occasional exigencies of his great design. But where there was no definite object he was not a tyrant.

The theory that he was a benevolent governor or a far-sighted statesman is not supported, either by the apparent purpose of his reforms, or by their actual result. It requires no particular benevolence to teach a king that his subjects are more contented when justice is fairly administered than when violence reigns unrepressed; and that where they are contented they are more likely to be industrious, and more able to pay taxes; that where they have more at stake they are more ready to make sacrifices to purchase security; but this is no lesson of far-sighted statesmanship, for it is the simplest principle of the art of government. If there were any sign of benevolence, any glimpse of the love of his people apparent in his actions, he ought by all means to have the credit of it; if there were any such general tone in his private life it might be allowed to give the key of interpretation of his public life, and a harmony to his whole character. But his life was violent and lawless; his personal design, wherever it clashed with his established measures, set them at once aside.

Again, such parts of his system as have been approved by the voice of late posterity, such as, especially, the restrictions on papal power and on ecclesiastical immunities, are capable of very simple discussion. There is no need to enter into a question of the personal merit of S. Thomas of Canterbury, or of the exact point for which he held out, and for which, in fact, he perished. We may respect the stout-heartedness of the prelate without approving his cause, or we may approve his cause without shutting our eyes to the violent and worldly spirit in which he conducted it; but when we find that in this cause all the piety and wisdom of three centuries saw the championship of Divine truth and justice against secular usurpation, we are not surely wrong in supposing that the Constitutions of Clarendon were dated three centuries too soon. Was Henry really three centuries before his age? If the answer is affirmative, we deny his character as a statesman, and reduce him to a theorist. In truth, it was as ancient customs that he wished to restore them, not to force them as innovations. His mistake was not that he anticipated the age of the Reformation, but that he neglected to consider that such was the rapid progress of papal assumption, and its acceptance, both in

England and on the continent, since the age of Hildebrand, that his "ancestral rights" were really left high and dry behind the advancing flood which he vainly thought to stem. The policy to which feudal antiquity had been forced to yield was really power-less against the increasing tide of ecclesiastical authority. The point which eluded the sagacity of Henry was identical with that which the Conqueror himself had overlooked when he established ecclesiastical courts to take cognisance of the secular offences of the clergy. Both saw the impossibility of reconciling royal su-premacy with the claims of feudal antiquity; but in ecclesiastical matters William yielded to, or perhaps helped on, the first trick-ling of the stream which Henry had to withstand in its full force. It was as necessary to William to strengthen as it was to Henry to weaken the power of the clergy. Henry should not have ex-pected to find in Becket one who would at once fill the seat and reverse the measures of Lanfranc.

In his secular and ecclesiastical reforms alike, he had an object to gain which demanded unusual measures; and he, without scru-ple and without remorse, tried to enforce them by all means, fair and foul. If he was not a mere tyrant, he was a man who was never deterred by any considerations but those of expediency from trying to win his game.

It seems, then, that there is a third and a truer reading of this eventful life, one which makes no demand on our credulity like the second, and which requires no harsh construction of simple actions like the first. Henry wished to create, at home and abroad, a strong government. In this itself there was nothing deserving the name of tyrannical; at the worst it was less of a tyranny than that which had been in use in the three Norman reigns, and had been exercised on both sides in the contests of that of Stephen. As governments were in those days, any might be accounted good which was conducted on the principle of law, not on ca-price. The notions of constitutional sovereignty and liberty were still locked up in the libraries, or in embryo in the brains of the clergy.

Such a theory makes Henry neither an angel nor a devil. He was a man of strong nature; strong will, strong affections, and strong passions. His ambition was not a wanton one. He began his reign without any temptation to be oppressive; but from the beginning we can read his purpose of being master in his own house. The humbling of the barons was no hard task; the initiation of law and order was an easy consequence; but the attempt to apply the principles of law and order to the clergy, in a way that was not sanctioned by the public opinion of his day, and which made his ablest counsellor his most inveterate foe, brought up an opposition which called into play all the violence of his nature. It was not that his character changed, but that circumstances brought out what was in him in a stronger light. After Becket's death, the circumstances became even stronger still, and brought out in a still stronger light the same characteristics.

By that most disastrous event all the elements of opposition were restored to life. Lewis had now a cause which, to his weak and wicked conscience, justified all the meanness and falsehood that he could use against his rival. The clergy dared not side with the king in such a quarrel. The barons took immediate advantage of the general disaffection. The king's sons lighted the flames of war. Not, I think, that there is any evidence to show that the death of S. Thomas was actually or nominally the pretext for revolt; but it was a breaking up of the restraints which had so far been effectual; and all who had grievances were ready and able to take advantage of the shock.

Under the circumstances, Henry did not show himself a hero, but he behaved as a moderate and politic conqueror. It was not revenge, but the restoration of the strength of his government that he desired. He did not break off his plans of reform: year after year saw some wise change introduced into the legal or military administration; and practically he managed the church without any glaring scandal. He ruled for himself, not for his people; but he did not rule cruelly or despotically. His character contained much that was tyrannical, but his policy was not such as to curse him with the name of tyrant.

15 *Frederick Pollock and Frederick William Maitland History of English Law*

To understand the Becket controversy it is essential to understand the place of ecclesiastical courts, "courts Christian" as they were called, and their claims to cognizance in the twelfth century. Two eminent legal historians, Frederick Pollock and Federick William Maitland, in their History of English Law, *describe the areas of conflict that existed between royal and episcopal jurisdiction.*

While this passage is strictly descriptive, it is easy to sense that legal minds of the late nineteenth century saw their champion as Henry, not Becket. Both Pollock and Maitland, but most particularly the latter, had mastered the details of medieval law, and they recognized that Henry "handed down to his successors a larger body of purely temporal justice than was to be found elsewhere."

The demarcation of the true province of ecclesiastical law was no easy task; it was not to be accomplished in England, in France, in Germany, without prolonged struggles. The Conqueror, when he ordained that "the episcopal laws" were not to be administered as of old in the hundred courts, left many questions open. During the first half of the twelfth century the claims of the church were growing, and the duty of asserting them passed into the hands of men who were not mere theologians but expert lawyers. Then, as all know, came the quarrel between Henry and Becket. In the Constitutions of Clarendon (1164) the king offered to the prelates a written treaty, a treaty which, so he said, embodied the "customs" of his ancestors, more especially of his grandfather. Becket, after some hesitation, rejected the constitutions. The dispute waxed hot; certain of the customs were condemned by the pope. The murder followed, and then Henry was compelled to renounce, though in carefully guarded

SOURCE. Frederick Pollock and Frederick William Maitland, *The History of English Law Before the Time of Edward I*, Vol. I, Boston: Little, Brown and Co., 1899, pp. 124-131.

terms, all his innovations. But his own assertion all along had been that he was no innovator; and though the honours and dishonours of the famous contest may be divided, the king was left in possession of the greater part of the field of battle. At two points he had been beaten:—the clerk suspected of felony could not be sentenced by, though he might be accused before, a lay court; appeals to Rome could not be prohibited, though in practice the king could, when he chose, do much to impede them. Elsewhere Henry had maintained his ground, and from his time onwards the lay courts, rather than the spiritual, are the aggressors and the victors in almost every contest. About many particulars we shall have to speak in other parts of our work; here we may take a brief survey of the province, the large province, which the courts Christian retain as their own.

The church claims cognizance of a cause for one of two reasons:—either because the matter in dispute is of an ecclesiastical or spiritual kind, or because the persons concerned in it, or some of them, are specially subject to the ecclesiastical jurisdiction.

I. (a) In the first place, she claims an exclusive cognizance of all affairs that can fairly be called matters of ecclesiastical economy, the whole law of ecclesiastical status, the ordination and degradation of clerks, the consecration of bishops, all purely spiritual functions such as the celebration of divine service, also the regulation of ecclesiastical corporations and the internal administration of their revenues. In this region the one limit set to her claims is the principle asserted by the state that the rights of the patrons (advocati) of churches are temporal rights, that the advowson (advocatio ecclesiae) is temporal property. To start with, the majority of churches had been owned by the landowners who built them. The spiritual power had succeeded in enforcing the rule that the "institution" of the clerk lies with the bishop; the choice of the clerk still lay with the landowner. Henry II maintained, Becket controverted, Alexander condemned this principle; but, despite papal condemnation, it seems to have been steadily upheld by the king's court, which prohibited the courts Christian from interfering with the right of patronage; and very soon we may find two prelates in litigation about an advowson before the royal justices. In this instance the clergy seem to have given way somewhat easily; both parties were at one in treating the advowson as a profitable, vendible right. Henry's victory at this point was of the utmost importance in after ages. It distinguishes England from other countries, and provides a base for anti-papal statutes. As regards other matters falling under the present head there was little debate; but it behooves us to notice that our temporal lawyers were thus excluded from some fruitful fields of jurisprudence. The growth of our law of corporations is slow, because our courts have nothing to do with the internal affairs of convents and chapters—the only institutions, that is, which seem to require treatment as fictitious persons; and we might have come by a law of trusts sooner than we did, if the justices had been bound to deal with the administration of revenues given to prelates or convents as a provision for particular purposes, such as the relief of the poor or the maintenance of fabrics.

(b) The ecclesiastical tribunals would much like to claim the decision of all causes which in any way concern those lands that have been given to a church, at all events if given by the way of "alms." Henry himself was willing to make what may seem to us a large concession at this point. If both parties agreed that the land had been given in alms, litigation about it was to proceed in the ecclesiastical forum; if they did not agree, then the preliminary question, which would decide where the case should be tried, was to be settled by the verdict of a jury. Here he was successful and much more than successful. The courts of his successors insisted on their exclusive right to adjudge all questions relating to the possession or ownership of land, albeit given in alms; the spiritual judges could in this province do no more than excommunicate for sacrilege one who invaded soil that had been devoted to God in the strictest sense by being consecrated.

(c) The courts Christian claimed the exaction of spiritual dues, tithes, mortuaries, oblations, pensions. The justice of the claim was not contested, but it was limited by the rule that a question about the title to the advowson is for the lay court. From century to century there was a border warfare over tithes between the two sets of lawyers, and from time to time some curious compromises were framed.

(d) More important is it for us to notice that the church claims marriage, divorce, and consequently legitimacy, as themes of ecclesiastical jurisdiction. This claim was not disputed by Henry II or his successors. However, the church in the twelfth century became definitely committed to the doctrine that children who were born out of wedlock were legitimated by the marriage of their parents. As regards the inheritance of land, a matter which lay outside the spiritual sphere, the king's courts would not accept this rule. The clergy endeavoured to persuade the lay power to bring its law into harmony with the law of the church, and then in the year 1236, as all know, the barons replied with one voice that they would not change the law of England. Thenceforward the king's justices assumed the right to send to a jury the question whether a person was born before or after the marriage of his parents, and it might well fall out that a man legitimate enough to be ordained or (it may be) to succeed to the chattels of his father, would be a bastard incapable of inheriting land either from father or from mother. But except when this particular question about the retroactive force of marriage arose, it was for the ecclesiastical court to decide the question of legitimacy, and, if this arose incidentally in the course of a temporal suit, it was sent for trial to the bishop and concluded by his certificate.

(e) Yet more important to us at the present day was another claim of the church, which has had the effect of splitting our English law of property into two halves. She claimed as her own the testament, that "last will" of a dead man which was intimately connected with his last confession. She claimed not merely to pronounce on the validity of wills, but also to interpret them, and also to regulate the doings of her creature the testamentary executor, whom she succeeded in placing alongside of the English heir. In the course of the thirteenth century the executor gradually becomes a prominent figure in the king's courts; he there sues the testator's debtors and is sued by his creditors; but the legatees who claim under the will must seek their remedies in the courts of the church. In this instance the common lawyers seem to have suffered the canonists to gradually enlarge a territory which was to be very valuable in the future. As a general rule, land could not be given by testament, and our king's court was concentrating its attention on land and crime. Meanwhile the church extends her boundaries, and at last succeeds in compassing the whole law of succession to movables *ab intestato*. The process whereby this was accomplished is very obscure; we shall speak of it upon another occasion; but here we may say that a notion prevailed that intestacy, if it be not exactly a sin, is often God's judgment on sin, for so closely is the last will connected with the last confession, that to die intestate is to die unconfessed. And so "the law of personal property" falls apart from "the law of real property" and we at this day are suffering from the consequences.

(f) With great difficulty were the courts Christian prevented from appropriating a vast region in the province of contract. They claimed to enforce—at the very least by spiritual censures—all promises made by oath, or by "pledge of faith." The man who pledges his faith, pawns his Christianity, puts his hopes of salvation in the hand of another. Henry II asserted his jurisdiction over such cases; Becket claimed at least a concurrent jurisdiction for the church. Henry was victorious. From his day onwards the royal court was always ready to prohibit ecclesiastical judges from entertaining a charge of breach of faith, unless indeed both parties to the contract were clerks, or unless the subject-matter of the promise was something that lay outside the jurisdiction of the temporal forum. All the same, there can be no doubt that during the whole of the next century the courts Christian were busy with breaches of faith. Very often a contractor expressly placed himself under their power and renounced all right to a prohibition. Such a renunciation was not fully effectual, for the right to issue the prohibition was the right of the king, not of the contractor; still, as Bracton explains, a man commits an enormous sin by seeking a prohibition when he has promised not to seek one and may very properly be sent to prison. In practice ecclesiastical judges were quite willing to run the risk of being prohibited; indeed the law of the church compelled them to take this hazard. A certain jurisdiction over marriage settlements of money or movable goods, the church had as part of its jurisdiction over marriage.

(g) There remains the indefinitely wide claim to correct the sinner for his soul's health, to set him some corporeal penance.

The temporal courts put a limit to this claim by asserting that, if the sin be also an offence which they can punish, the spiritual judges are not to meddle with it. There are some few exceptions; the bodies of the clergy are doubly protected; you may be put to penance for laying violent hands upon a clerk besides being imprisoned for the breach of the peace and having to pay damages for the trespass. But even though this rule be maintained, much may be done for the correction of sinners. The whole province of sexual morality is annexed by the church; she punishes fornication, adultery, incest; and these offences are not punished by the king's court, though the old local courts are still exacting *legerwites* and *childwites*, fines for fornication. So also the province of defamation is made over to the spiritual jurisdiction, for, though the local courts entertain actions for slander and libel, the king's court, for some reason or another, has no punishment for the defamer, no relief for the defamed. Usury is treated as a mere sin while the usurer is living; but if he dies in sin, the king seizes his goods. Simony naturally belongs to the church courts; perjury, not always well distinguished from the breach of a promissory oath, would come before them upon many occasions, though with perjured jurors the royal court could deal. Of heresy we need as yet say nothing, for England had hardly been troubled by heretics. No doubt the church courts were quite prepared to deal with heresy should it raise its head, and had they called upon the state to burn or otherwise punish the heretic, it is not likely that they would have called in vain.

II. (a) But the church had opened a second parallel. She claimed cognizance of all personal causes, criminal or civil, in which a clerk was the accused or the defendant. The story of "the benefit of clergy" we shall tell elsewhere. On the whole, save in one particular, the state had its way. The clerk accused of felony was to be tried in the ecclesiastical court and was to suffer no other punishment than that which the ecclesiastical court could inflict; it could inflict lifelong imprisonment. But whatever may have been the case in the twelfth century, the clerk of the thirteenth can be tried and punished for all his minor offences as though he were a layman. Then again, in Bracton's day the clerk has no privilege when he is defendant in a civil action, though in the past clerks have been allowed to sue each other for debts and the like in courts Christian. It should be well understood that "the benefit of clergy" as allowed by English law was but a small part of that general immunity from lay justice which was claimed for the ordained by canonists in England as well as elsewhere.

(b) On the continent of Europe the church often claimed as her own the suits of the *miserabiles personae*, as they were called, of widows and orphans. Of any such claim we hear little or nothing in England, though some tradition of it may affect the later history of the Court of Chancery. In England it is the king who sets feudal rules aside in order that summary justice may be done to the widow.

Large then is the province of ecclesiastical law; but it might have been much larger. Despite the many advantages that Henry II gave to his antagonists by his rages and his furies, he handed down to his successors a larger field of purely temporal justice than was to be found elsewhere. Even in Normandy Richard had to consign to the ecclesiastical forum all questions about broken oath or broken faith. But we are here concerned with the fact that from the middle of the twelfth century onwards a very large mass of litigation, of litigation to which in no very strict sense can be called ecclesiastical, was handed over to tribunals which administered the canon law, tribunals which were often constituted by a papal rescript, and from which there lay an appeal to the Roman curia.

PART FOUR

Twentieth Century Views

TWENTIETH CENTURY VIEWS
INTRODUCTION

Dom David Knowles offers a clue to an understanding of the contributions made by historians of this century to the subject of this book when he writes:

"The celebrated conflict between Henry II and Archbishop Thomas of Canterbury has received comparatively little attention from English historians in the past fifty years. . . . A feeling developed that the topic had been exhausted, and even that it was a sterile one"[1]

His own writing thoroughly disproves his fear that the subject is indeed sterile, and a few other writers have managed to squeeze additional substance from it, but they have done so without the passion and flair of their nineteenth-century predecessors.

Mme. Foreville revived the issues in a thorough study, part of which is quoted below. Most of the serious scholars of the twentieth century have tended to support the king rather than the archbishop. Barlow and Knowles, as well as others, have introduced judiciously balanced interpretations.

[1] Dom David Knowles, *The Episcopal Colleagues of Thomas Becket*, University Press, Cambridge, 1951, p. 7.

16   *Raymonde Foreville*
      Church and State in England Under Henry II

*One of the personalities most involved in the controversy was
Thomas's counterpart, the archbishop of York, Roger of Pont-
l'Évêque. Roger, whose acquaintance with Thomas began when both
were young clerks on the staff of Theobald at Canterbury, felt personal as well as professional hostility toward Becket.*

Mme. Raymonde Foreville, author of L'Église et la Royauté en
Angleterre sous Henri II Plantagenet *(Church and State in England
Under Henry II Plantagenet), suggests in the following passage that
this rivalry and the hostility of Gilbert Foliot, bishop of London,
toward the archbishop of Canterbury, helped to keep the bitterness
of the affair smoldering. Her analysis of the jurisdictional claims of
the king may be compared to Pollock and Maitland's discussion of
the same topic.*

The first acts of Thomas of Canterbury's pontificate demon-
strated both his resolution to dedicate himself solely to the duties
of his post and his desire to restore to the primatial church its dignities and prerogatives. Freed from all compromise with secular
authority, he sought the support of the Roman church in spite
of the schism that was then lacerating it. From the time of his
elevation to the see of Canterbury he had pressed Alexander III
regarding his claim to the pallium; the pope, in flight from the
triumphant troops of Barbarosa, landed on the coast of France
and sent the pallium through envoys of the archbishop of Montpellier during the month of July 1162. Thomas Becket received
it in his cathedral on August 10, barefoot and unadorned by
pontifical vestments in token of his deference toward the Roman
authority. In the following year the pope convoked a general

SOURCE. Raymonde Foreville, *L'Église et la Royauté en Angleterre sous
Henri II Plantaganet*, translated by Thomas Jones, Paris: Bloud & Gay,
1943, pp. 115–121. Reprinted by permission of the publisher.

council at Tours, in Plantagenet territory, with the approval of
Henry and of the king of France. The archbishop obtained from
the king, for himself and for his episcopal colleagues, permission
to leave the kingdom and answer the summons of the pope. Upon
his approach to the city where the council was soon to open,
the primate of England was welcomed both by the crowd of
people who had recently acclaimed him as chancellor of Henry
II, and by a multitude of ecclesiastical dignitaries. The pope himself greeted Thomas with the greatest cordiality. The council
restored the fidelity of the bishops to the cause of Alexander III.
It renewed a certain number of canonical regulations that had
become a dead letter perhaps even more in England than on the
continent; it was principally concerned with stopping the alienation of ecclesiastical property for the profit of laymen. The
battles of the reign of Stephen had multipled such alienation in
England; the church of Ely suffered, and even the church of
Canterbury was not exempt; the chief of the Flemish merce-
naries, William of Ypres, had usurped and kept some important
fiefs in the county of Kent. The council of Tours effectively
directed Thomas Becket toward a sense of devotion to the interests of the Roman church and to the interests of the church
of Canterbury, which solidly supported him. Upon his return to
England he soon adapted his attitude so that it conformed to the
prescriptions of the council, including both the recommendations
of the pope and the view of the cardinals who were most firmly
committed to the cause of Alexander III and the rights of the
Roman church. It was then that he formed deep friendships with
Cardinal Humbold of Ostia, one of the abler collaborators of
Adrian IV, and with Conrad, archbishop-elect of Mainz.

Consistent with the canonical regulations just restored to practice at Tours, Thomas Becket upon his return to the kingdom
determined to take back in full the domain lands of Canterbury
which had been alienated under his predecessors: he reclaimed
from the king the castles of Rochester, Saltwood, and Hythe,
treading the path beaten by Anselm, who had recovered lands
lost by his two immediate predecessors and who had urged his
successors to conserve the ecclesiastical domain. In the name of
justice he opposed policies such as the privilege of diverting the
sheriff's aid into a royal levy, an aid which up to that time had

been voluntarily granted by ecclesiastical and lay barons to the sheriff so that he could maintain order and public safety.

Thoroughly understanding all the consequences of such an attitude, pressed moreover by ambitious counsellors whose envy and vindictiveness had been aroused by the chancellor's rapid promotion, Henry II reclaimed, or allowed his barons and officials to reclaim, the exercise of certain seignorial rights and certain royal prerogatives, thus attacking the archbishop on his own ground both as a feudal and an ecclesiastical lord. It is in this light that one must see the refusal of Roger, count of Clare and a vassal of the church of Canterbury, to do homage to the archbishop for the castle of Tunbridge, and his claim that he held it from no one except the king. A lay lord, William of Eynesford, then expelled the vicar who had been installed by Thomas in a church within William's fief, reclaiming the right of patronage and carrying to the court of the king the case against the excommunication that the archbishop had imposed upon him. In the name of crown prerogatives Henry II proclaimed that he was opposed to ecclesiastical sentences which could be directed against his own barons without his authorization, since he had not made the judgment himself. Finally, upon his order sheriffs summoned to their own courts certain clerks accused of crime: a canon of Bedford, Philip of Brois, who had been found innocent of the murder of a knight by the bishop of Lincoln, was forced to answer to a sheriff for the same crime. Furious at finding himself brought before a secular court, he lost his temper and injured the royal officer. The archbishop did not let this crime pass unpunished; he deprived the clerk of his title and of the revenues from his prebend, and banished him from the kingdom for two years. Ready to render justice or to demand it of his suffragans, Thomas Becket opposed the summoning of other criminous clerks before secular courts, claiming the tribunal privilege prescribed by the canons, instituted in England by the Conqueror and considerably strengthened by actual practice in the middle of the twelfth century.

Those rights which the English primate claimed for the church, Henry Plantagenet tried to secure for the crown through agreement on the part of the barons assembled in the royal council at Westminster 1 October 1163. Without reviewing the particular cases of accused clerks, the king complained in general of crimes commited by clergymen over a period of years and of the excessive indulgence of episcopal courts in their behalf. He demanded that in the future every defrocked clerk must be brought to his court for sentencing, according to the penalty of common law related to the crime that he had committed.

The kings always had reserved for themselves cognizance of certain crimes and had kept for themselves some control over the exercise of episcopal justice; in general, this arrangement had been developing in English practice since the Conqueror. While it was debatable from a canonical point of view, English usage had indirectly and over a long period of time resulted in the disappearance of canonical privileges. Further, this usage constituted a real menace to the independence of ecclesiastical justice. Thomas of Canterbury opposed the royal will in the name of canonical principles and clerical immunity:

"Over the heritage of Jesus Christ the secular power has stretched its hand, from the viewpoint of the sainted Fathers' decrees; the canonical decrees, whose very name is odious in our land, are powerless to protect the clerks who up to now, through special exemption, have been immune from secular jurisdiction."[1]

The episcopate supported the archbishop in his reasoned resistance. The question then seemed closed due to his justified opposition; in fact, hostilities were re-opened only between the king and the primate. Now Henry's attempt to restore royal control over the administration of justice in the church largely went beyond the accepted limits of the English monarchy. The isolated episodes of 1163, prelude to a conflict of far-reaching magnitude, already had assumed their full significance, if one may judge from the example of analogous measures which the king imposed in certain continental provinces of the Angevin empire. Since 1158, in England itself, on the advice of Richard de Lucy, Henry Plantagenet had refused to defer to the archbishop of York in the case of a dean found guilty of collecting heavy fines during the exercise of his judicial functions, and

[1] *Materials for the History of Thomas Becket*, Vol. V, pp. 48–9.

he was summoned to his court; the death of Geoffrey of Anjou had occurred unexpectedly in the interval and probably the intervention of the chancellor had stopped the king from execution of his summons. In 1159, in an ordinance drawn up at Falaise, the king expressed his dissatisfaction with the manner in which archdeacons and deans handled justice, and he instituted in Normandy the accusing jury in criminal matters. More recently, in the month of February 1162, Henry II, holding his court at Rouen, had energetically restored in the duchy of Normandy the old practices dating back to the Conqueror, introduced at the council of Lillebonne (1180) and renewed under Henry I. The decisions of Lillebonne established the jurisdiction of the ducal court in certain cases relating to clerks, such as the possession of land, the forest law, and constraint if such were necessary so that justice might be rendered by the bishop. In spite of a certain indefiniteness that failed to remove doubts left by the obscurity of an epoch when the Norman practice was still notorious, the canons of Lillebonne sanctioned the existence and the jurisdiction of church courts, both civil and criminal. The exigencies of Henry II at Rouen we can only know from his simple reference to the council of 1080; one can infer nevertheless that there was a question of retracting the extension of ecclesiastical jurisdiction over matters of property and of its seizure out of preference for the ducal court. Finally in 1163 the Plantagenet king tried to obtain a commitment from the bishop of Poitiers, John of Belmeis, that the bishop would renounce on his part certain judicial privileges of the church; according to the terms of the royal order cited by the justiciar, Richard de Lucy, the bishop should surrender to the king rights over land litigation concerning widows, orphans, clerks, and cases of usury; he should renounce also the right to invoke anathema upon barons of the crown without royal consent; penalties such as the confiscation of goods and imprisonment were imposed upon all those, clergy or laity, who still tried to use episcopal courts in the listed cases. The bishop of Poitiers, a friend of Thomas Becket, opposed the royal attempt for the same reasons the primate of England had used. Only the docile Norman bishops appear to have accepted the royal injunctions without resistance, surrendering the prerogatives they had enjoyed for a considerable length of time under Stephen of Blois

and Geoffrey Plantagenet. Henry II hoped in the course of the
years 1162 and 1163 to recover the rights that his predecessors
had allowed to lapse in Normandy, and to unify judicial practices
in all the territories under his domination for the enhancement
of royal power. Doubtless the promotion of the chancellor to
the primate's office was a part of a plan to return the English
church to subservience.

But there was more to come. The conflict which kept Thomas
Becket and Henry II in opposition for seven years had a double
origin: on the one hand the king tried to reduce the privileges of
the English clergy and contain them strictly within the frame-
work of the feudal state, the direction of which he intended to
recover and protect; on the other hand, the openly hostile episcopate, jealous of the rapid elevation of the chancellor who at
the beginning had made common cause with the king, was quick
to align itself with the king's supporter's. In his enterprise, which
was an integral part of a vast legislative and judicial reform, the
Plantagenet would be supported not only by his officials, but
further by the jealousy, the ambition, and the servility of certain
fawning prelates, principally Gilbert Foliot. Then very prominent for his reputation of integrity and erudition, the bishop of
Hereford was transferred to London by papal authorization
upon the express demand of Henry II, whose wish had once
again prevented regular election by the chapter. The primate,
solicited by the king, had agreed to this promotion and had commended to the pope the royal request and that of the church of London. Thus accord of the interested powers was achieved: the king,
the chapter, the metropolitan, and the papacy, whose intervention
was considered indispensible in order to proceed with the transfer
of a bishop from one see to another. In the course of the first
two years of his term as archbishop, even though he had encountered difficulties elsewhere, Thomas Becket had assured the
canonical elections of the vacant sees in agreement with the king:
after London, Hereford, where the celebrated professor Robert
of Melun, apparently the candidate of the archbishop, was promoted; and Worcester was filled by the nomination of Roger,
son of the count of Gloucester and cousin of the Plantagenet
king. The archbishop consecrated them in his own cathedral on
22 December 1163 and 23 August 1164 respectively. Neverthe-

less the new prelates were not slow to detach themselves from their metropolitan. Only Roger of Worcester, in spite of his relationship to the royal house, rallied early to the cause of Thomas Becket.

Reviewing the origin of the conflict the archbishop of Canterbury was moved to write much later that the bishop of London

has strengthened the heart and the arm of the king and of his officials, then he has assisted in a similar way our brother and friend the archbishop of York, and through his ingenuity has turned away certain of our brothers from their mother the church of Canterbury, to whom they owe out of respect for their profession loyalty and obeisance, so that they would write to the lord the pope in support of the archbishop of York (since his promotion he has not ceased to use all his power and all his skill to extend his snares toward the church of Canterbury which has nourished him), urging the pope to allow the archbishop to carry his cross, rival of the true cross but planted on a trunk of arrogance, traversing our province in order to appear to have reached a kind of equality with the church of Canterbury.[2]

Then, at the same time when the primate saw himself obliged to defend against the will of the king the unwritten laws of the English church, for which he considered himself chiefly responsible, his own suffragans deserted his cause and the archbishop reopened the secular conflict between the two metropolitans.

In fact, Roger of Pont-l'Évêque, clerk and archdeacon of Canterbury, promoted to the see of York with the backing of Theobald's influence, had already set himself up against the person who had been his spiritual father: in the absence of the archbishop he had undertaken the pretension of placing the crown upon the royal head at the solemn court held at Lincoln at Christmas 1157. The intervention of the clerk of Theobald, John of Salisbury, and John of Belmeis, then treasurer of York, who were close to the chancellor and the king, dissuaded Henry II from such a project and the ceremony was to be performed

[2] Materials, Vol. VI, p. 590.

instead by the bishop of Lincoln, a suffragan of the primatial church.

Meanwhile, the archbishop of York had claimed at the council of Tours, his own primacy over Thomas of Canterbury on the basis of his earlier consecration. This primacy does not appear to have been granted; at least Alexander III decided to reserve the respective rights of the two English archbishops, invoking as an excuse the smallness of the church of St. Maurice, where the council was taking place, smallness which did not permit the strict respect required for the archbishop's presence. Subsequently Roger of Pont-l'Évêque multiplied the affronts toward his colleague: called upon to travel frequently in the southern province to assist the king through his counsel, Roger went there as an aggressor, ostentatiously ordering his archiepiscopal cross to be carried before him. To the protests of Thomas Becket he responded through an appeal to the pope, summoning the archbishop of Canterbury to appear before the tribunal of the Apostle (October 1163).

The first ten years of Henry II's reign had been marked by a general restoration of royal power in which the church of Canterbury had participated significantly under Archbishop Theobald and Archdeacon Thomas of London, who was promoted to chancellor of the kingdom. One or the other of them, along with Adrian IV, kept trying vigorously to persuade the king toward a viewpoint sympathetic to the prerogatives of the apostolic see and of the English primatial see. Meanwhile their action imprinted itself upon the entire dissembling character of the new king, who was jealous of lesser manifestations of prestige and authority. Occasionally Thomas Becket had succeeded by his personal influence in restraining that impulsive temperament, irascible and authoritarian, which the adulation of the courtiers and the counsel of the justiciars rendered daily more demanding about the rights of the crown. Far from strengthening the royal attack upon the English church in line with Plantagenet designs, the elevation of the chancellor to the primatial see put him clearly in a position to protect the liberties which the justiciars had previously tried hard to reduce throughout the entire Plantagenet empire, especially in judicial matters. Very skillfully the king and his counsellors proceeded to win to their cause the archbishop of York, episcopal rival of the primate of England, in the process reviving the old quarrel of the metropolitans and one important faction of the suffragan episcopate of Canterbury. In October 1163, the council of Westminster and Roger of Pont-l'Évêque's appeal to Rome marked the beginning of a long conflict with a double face: opposition of the king and the primate over the question of the dignity of the crown and the rights of the church, plus opposition of the two metropolitans of England regarding the respective claims of their churches. That double conflict, essentially judicial, would soon tear apart the church and the monarchy of England, provoke the death of the primate and, for ten years more, suspend the application of great judicial reforms of the reign, ultimately obliging Henry II to consult the Roman church about his methods of reform. It would lead the two parties to agree to mutual concessions, and finally exercise a considerable influence upon the subsequent evolution of ecclesiastical law and of royal custom in England.

## 17					*Dom David Knowles*
The Episcopal Colleagues of Thomas Becket

The Reverend David Knowles has managed to bring to life both the drama and the issues that reached their climax at the Northampton meeting of the royal council. Several earlier selections have discussed the Clarendon meetings, but it was at Northampton that the king finally made it clear that he was out to destroy Becket, and that Becket decided that his only course was to escape from the kingdom and live as an archbishop-in-exile. There is probably no better-balanced description of the events of Northampton than this one.

SOURCE. David Knowles, *The Episcopal Colleagues of Archbishop Thomas Becket*, New York: Cambridge University Press, 1951, pp. 66–73, 76–79, 85–88. Reprinted by permission of the publisher and the author.

The assembly at Northampton, which was convoked for 6th October, 1164, differed in many respects from the council at Clarendon. At the latter the archbishops and bishops, forming a body of considerable solidarity, had been as a group the object of attack on an issue of high ecclesiastical policy—the conduct of the courts and relations with Rome. At Northampton the issue was ostensibly one of royal justice only. The bishops were present simply as normal members of the great Council, and, since the archbishop's double *volte-face* at Clarendon and after, they had become a group without a leader rather than a body with a head. At the same time, many of them must have been uneasy at their submission and secretly in approval of their archbishop's latest position, though not, perhaps, of his impulsive and, it may have seemed, secretive conduct.

Few gatherings in medieval history are more rich in moral and dramatic interest or have been recorded in greater wealth of detail than the council of Northampton. We have at least seven long narratives and a number of shorter accounts, and of the seven two at least are the work of men who were present at the archbishop's side throughout. As is to be expected, there are numerous disagreements and discrepancies in detail, some of which are not susceptible of resolution, and while on the whole we must follow the two eye-witnesses, William FitzStephen and Herbert of Bosham, who, especially when they agree, have every claim on our belief, yet several of the others add numerous facts, from whatever sources they may come, which explain or support the two principal narratives.

On the first day on which the assembly got down to business, Thursday, 8th October, there was a long discussion, at the end of which the archbishop was judged to be guilty of contempt of the royal jurisdiction in having neglected to obey the royal summons to court, and to have forfeited all his movable goods to the king's mercy. When, however, it came to pronouncing sentence a difficulty arose, neither the barons nor the bishops wishing to shoulder the responsibility. The barons complained that they were mere laymen, while the bishops retorted that this was a secular, not an ecclesiastical, court, and that they, the bishops, could not be asked to condemn their superior. Finally the king insisted that all should take part, and laid the obligation of pronouncing sentence on the bishop of Winchester. The archbishop at first refused to acknowledge the court, but in the end submitted. He was judged to have forfeited all his movable goods to the king, and all the bishops became his guarantors, with the significant exception of the bishop of London.

The day had undoubtedly been one of success for the king. The archbishop had been encountered on a terrain where his canonical foothold was slippery; he had at first taken a high line and then yielded. Similarly the bishops, bound by feudal loyalty and the Clarendon oath, had at first writhed and then given way, thus losing the advantage of a gracious compliance with the king, while becoming awkwardly embroiled with their chief. The guarantee which they gave on the archbishop's behalf was an attempt to satisfy another loyalty, but here, too, neither king nor archbishop would give them any thanks. Henry would probably have been well advised, had peace been his genuine desire, to rest upon his success and dismiss all thoughts of further charges against the archbishop. That, however, it was not in the king's character to do.

The logical sequel to the condemnation of the archbishop for contempt of the king's summons to his court would have been the trial before Henry of the case of John the Marshal, whose appeal from the archbishop's jurisdiction had provided the king with a useful weapon. Here, however, Henry was on weak ground. The archbishop's judgment had probably been just, the Marshal had avoided perjury only by a subterfuge, and the sympathy of all the great lords of honors was with the holder of a baronial court. Henry therefore dropped the case, and was for reviving the issue of criminous clerks, but his advisers pointed out that this would reunite the bishops and their metropolitan, so the king proceeded to a series of demands that were frankly punitive. The first of these was for money received from the castelleries of Eye and Berkhampstead. No previous notice had been given of this and the money had been spent in the royal service, but the archbishop, still hoping for peace, accepted the obligation, for which three lay barons stood guarantors. The king's next demand was for large sums borrowed by the chancellor for the siege of Toulouse and other purposes; the king claimed that these were a pure loan and pressed for judgment. Once more the bishops were forced to condemn their leader, and once more lay-men, five in number, stood as guarantors. But it was not money, nor even a forensic triumph, that Henry wanted; he wanted to break the archbishop, and he now demanded accounts for all receipts from vacant bishoprics, including Canterbury, and abbeys held by the chancellor during his term of office. This was of course a wholly outrageous demand. The moneys had in fact been the equivalent of revenue, received and spent by a royal official, and the absence of any adverse comment either at the time or later would in itself have been in equity equivalent to a discharge, even if this had not been, as Thomas alleged, formally given. Moreover, the archbishop was now legally penniless, with all his friends deeply engaged on his behalf. Further obligations could only have meant imprisonment or the dismemberment of the archbishopric. Thomas demanded time for counsel with his colleagues, and the meeting broke up on the Friday evening. The following days were occupied with ceaseless negotiations, and it is not surprising that the accounts present numerous difficulties. Fortunately, the two eye-witnesses, FitzStephen and Herbert of Bosham, give the fullest accounts, and with numerous indications of time and day. They are not always in perfect agreement; Herbert wrote many years after the events, and we can follow FitzStephen with more assurance.

The demand for accounts had been made on Friday, 9th October. On the morning of Saturday all the prelates came to the archbishop's lodging at St. Andrew's, and he consulted both bishops and abbots separately. Of the abbots' counsel nothing is known, but the speeches of the bishops have been reported in some detail. Although the accounts are at variance, it must have been at this first meeting that the archbishop repeated that he had been given full quittance on the king's behalf on the day of his consecration. Henry of Winchester, the consecrator, now he came to think about it, remembered the incident clearly; it was in fact common knowledge, and the bishops in a body waited upon the king to remind him of this. Henry, however, refused to be put off, whereupon the bishop of Winchester, to whom money was no object, tried an offer on his own of 2,000 marks. But it was not cash that the king wanted—indeed, as the event showed, he was no longer working to a rational plan at all. Once more the bishops took counsel with their head. It is at this point that one of the biographers, who was not himself present or even in England at the time, but who nevertheless had access to good sources, inserts a short summary of the advice given to Thomas by his colleagues.

Gilbert Foliot, as dean of the province, began by reminding the archbishop of his lowly origin, of the royal benefactions to him, and of the ruin to which he was bringing the Church in England. He therefore advised resignation. Henry of Winchester, the father of the bench, took a different view. The archbishop's resignation, he thought, would set a most pernicious example. In the future, any prelate who had a difference with the king would have to resign. Canon law, not personal or political considerations, must be the decisive criterion. Hilary of Chichester followed. The advice of the bishop of Winchester, he said, was excellent for ordinary times, but in the present predicament everything was at sixes and sevens, and a prudent economizing was more likely to win through than a rigid adherence to the canons. He therefore advised a discreet submission, which would be better than a forced retreat from an extreme position. After him came Robert of Lincoln, characterized as a simple and indiscreet man. To him the matter was plain. The king, he said, was seeking the archbishop's life, and what good would the archbishopric be to a dead man? Bartholomew of Exeter followed: the days were evil, he said, and only by a compromise could the storm be weathered. The present attack of the king was personal and not general; the archbishop must be sacrificed rather than the whole Church. Finally Roger, the elect of Worcester, was asked his opinion, but refused to give it explicitly. To counsel the archbishop's resignation would be against his conscience, he said; to advise resistance to the king would be to put himself at the bar with his metropolitan. Whatever the historical accuracy of these declarations, the general impression of indecision and lack of firm support for the archbishop may be taken as a fair reflection of the prevailing frame of mind. Archbishop Thomas, we are told, decided to temporize, and sent the bishops of London and Rochester to the king with the message that those who knew most about the accounts were not yet at Northampton, but that on the next day of the council he would answer as God might

show him. Foliot, according to one account, did his best to com-
mit the archbishop by conveying the message in a different form:
the archbishop, he announced, requested a brief delay in order
to present his accounts. When, however, the Earls of Leicester
and Cornwall came to say that the king would agree if that was
indeed the reason for delay, the archbishop disclaimed all responsibility for the message in that form. He would come, he
said, God helping, and would answer as it should be given him. . . .

The scenes of the following day, Tuesday, 13th October, are
among the most celebrated in English domestic history. The
archbishop, against all expectation, had recovered; he was visited
in the early morning by agitated bishops who had heard that trial
and condemnation as a traitor were awaiting him; the general
advice was that he should resign and submit himself unreservedly
to the king. The archbishop replied with bitter force: "The sons
of my own mother have fought against me." During the past
days, he added, the bishops, instead of supporting him, had twice
given judgment against him in a civil case; now he feared that
they would do the same on a criminal count. This he forbade
them to do under pain of suspension, and appealed to Rome
against them. Moreover, he commanded them to excommunicate
forthwith any who should lay violent hands upon him. As for
himself, he would stand firm. While the others heard this in silence, Gilbert Foliot immediately lodged a counter-appeal against
the archbishop's last command; the bishops then left St. Andrew's
for the castle, save for two, who remained for a few minutes to
express their sympathy for the archbishop and to hearten him.
The two were Henry of Winchester and Jocelin of Salisbury.

The archbishop then celebrated Mass with its significant Introit
Etenim sederunt principes and its still more significant gospel with
its reference to Zachary slain between the temple and the altar.
Then, still wearing some of the priestly vestments under a cloak,
preceded by his cross, and carrying secretly the sacred Host to
serve as Viaticum should the worst befall, he took horse for the
castle. Then took place a famous incident. Dismounting in the
court-yard, as the gate shut behind him, he took from his bearer
the archiepiscopal cross. Some bishops were at the door of the
castle, among them Gilbert of London. One of the archbishop's
clerks, Hugh of Nunant, later bishop of Conventry, approached

him: "My Lord of London, can you stand by while the archbishop carries his own cross?" "My dear fellow," replied Foliot,
"the man always was a fool and he'll be one till he dies." Robert
of Hereford, his old master, tried to take the cross from him in
vain; Foliot, approaching on the other side, told the archbishop
sharply that he was a fool, and he also endeavoured to wrest the
cross from him. Roger of Worcester rebuked Foliot: "Would
you prevent your Lord from carrying his cross?", only to be
told sharply that he would live to be sorry for those words. The
bishops then fell aside and Thomas entered alone, bearing his cross,
and passed through the hall himself; the others followed, and
Foliot again remonstrated: "Let one of your clerks carry it."
Thomas refused. "Then let me have it; I am your dean; do you
not realize that you are threatening the king? If you take your
cross and the king draws his sword how can we ever make peace
between you?" "The cross is the sign of peace," answered
Thomas. "I carry it to protect myself and the English Church."

The wrangle over, the bishops drew away from the archbishop,
who had now entered the inner chamber, and he sat alone, with
two clerks, who were to be his biographers, at his feet, waiting
for the worst that could happen. At this tense moment a touch
of bitter comedy, not unobserved by one of the clerks, was
provided by the entrance of Roger of York. He had arrived late
to the council, partly to ensure attention, like a queen at the thea-
tre, partly, so the chronicler suggests, to have a secure alibi should
he be charged with having worked the archbishop's downfall.
He now entered, with his unpermitted cross borne before him,
and there were thus two crosses in the castle as it were two hostile
lances at rest. The bishops were then summoned to council with
the king, who had retreated to the upper floor at the news of
Thomas's advent.

*　*　*

The climax of the long day was now at hand. The archbishop
was seated, holding his cross. With him sat his suffragans, who,
as a body, had appealed to the Pope against him. In an upper
room, near enough for the angry cries of "Traitor!" to be heard
by those below, were gathered the barons, stiffened by the addi-

tion of the sheriffs and lesser men. In such a gathering the issue was certain, and the archbishop was condemned and sentenced— to what, never appeared, but probably to that perpetual imprisonment which he most dreaded. While the king and a few others remained, the main body of the council came down the stairs to pronounce sentence. The archbishop did not rise to meet them, but remained seated, still holding the cross. Proceedings did not begin at once, as none of the leaders of the council was anxious to act as spokesman; some still had sympathy with the archbishop; still more had Regan's dread of a spiritual father's malediction. These men, it must be remembered, were not the fawning time-servers, the Riches and Audleys, who surrounded Henry VIII, but the founders of abbeys and the friends of saints.

Finally, after the duty had been passed round, the Earl of Leicester, a man of good report with all the biographers, took up the unwelcome tale. He began with a long recital of the archbishop's debt of gratitude to the king, and passed on to a minute account of the events at Clarendon. It was clear that he feared to come to the point. The archbishop saw his opportunity; breaking in on the earl, he forbade anyone present to pass judgment on him. Leicester was shaken, but began again, still more slowly, then exclaimed that he would not do it, and bade the Earl of Cornwall take his place. He too boggled, whereupon Hilary of Chichester, to expedite matters, said that the treason was clear, and bade the archbishop hear the judgment. Thomas rose, exclaiming that it was none of their business to judge their archbishop, and strode through the hall towards the door. There was an uproar, some calling him traitor, others gesticulating and hurling rushes and other débris into the air. In the press, the archbishop stumbled over a cord of faggots by the central hearth and there was more shouting and jeering. Hamelin, the king's illegitimate half-brother, again shouted "Traitor!"; Thomas, turning on him, gave him the lie as a lout and a bastard. "If I were not a priest," he exclaimed, "my hands should prove my honour on you." And thus, in the biographer's phrase they departed from the council. The gate of the bailey was locked, but the porter was scuffling with a private enemy, a bunch of keys hung on the wall unguarded, and a clerk found the right one. Thomas rode across the town acclaimed by the people.

There was no pursuit. According to one biographer Roger of York and Foliot immediately advised the king to take no violent step in the crowded and excited town, but to send for the archbishop at some future date and imprison him; according to another, it was Robert of Hereford who represented to the king that any violence would prejudice his cause. Actually, perhaps, the attack on the archbishop, like a cavalry charge, had got out of hand and overswept its objective, and Thomas's unexpected move had nonplussed his opponents. In any case Henry made proclamation that the archbishop was not to be molested, though we need not take too seriously Foliot's later account of Henry as another David, begging his knights to save him the boy Absalom.

18   *Count Ugo Balzani*
Frederick Barbarossa and the Lombard League

Diplomacy involving the Holy Roman Empire, France, England, and the papacy formed a moving backdrop for the twelfth century events of the English church. The emperor, Frederick I (called Barbarossa for the color of his beard), inherited from a line of predecessors dating back to Otto I a policy of trying to unite Germany and Italy under a single rule. He also inherited a bitter struggle between the pro-papal Guelf forces in Germany and the pro-imperial Ghibelline forces, led by his own Hohenstaufen family.

Frederick's reign, from 1152 to 1190, coincided almost exactly with Henry II's. His conflict with Alexander III, who supported the Lombard towns in their opposition to the emperor, caused him to support a series of antipopes. Alexander was forced into exile. This circumstance, added to the continued presence of a rival pope, forced him to be circumspect in his support of the archbishop of Canterbury. Nevertheless, Frederick could not count on winning Henry as an ally, as Alexander well knew. Henry was committed to Guelf alli-

SOURCE. Count Ugo Balzani, "Frederick Barbarossa and the Lombard League," in H. M. Gwatkin and J. P. Whitney, eds., *The Cambridge Medieval History*, Vol. V, London: Cambridge University Press and New York: Macmillan Company, 1926, pp. 433–439. Reprinted by permission of the publisher.

ance through the marriage of his daughter to Frederick's German opponent, Henry the Lion.

In the following selection from The Cambridge Medieval History, *the author credits Alexander with both skill and forcefulness in the tangled diplomacy. He clearly disagrees with those who argue that the pope acted in timid vacillation during the years of the Becket case. The battles over the Lombard town, remote as they were from Canterbury, were not isolated from the turmoil over the English archbishop.*

Frederick at last had brought Crema to surrender, and had given orders for the demolition of the heroic city and the dispersal of the citizens. In February 1160 he opened the Synod of Pavia with an oration in which, notwithstanding the vagueness of the phraseology, his thoughts concerning the relations of the Empire and the Church were transparent enough. "Although," he said, "in my office and dignity of Emperor I can convoke councils, especially in moments of peril for the Church, as did Constantine, Theodosius, Justinian, and in later times the Emperors Charlemagne and Otto, yet we leave it to your prudence and power to decide in this matter. God made you priests and gave you power to judge us also. And since it is not for us to judge you in things appertaining to God, we exhort you so to act in this matter as though we awaited from you the judgment of God." Thus speaking he retired, leaving the Council to their deliberations. At this Council were assembled many abbots and lesser ecclesiastics, but only fifty of the rank of bishop and archbishop, the majority of whom were Germans or northern Italians. From other countries hardly any had come, and some foreign sovereigns had sent in adhesions[1] couched in vague terms which were received and registered as if they had a positive value. Octavian had no difficulty in establishing the validity of his cause, all the more so since Alexander was not present, owing to his refusal to recognize the synod, and thus did nothing to vindicate his case. Alexander besides had to reckon with the accusation of his hostility to the Empire and alliance with the Sicilians and the Lombards. Octavian was acknowledged to be Pope and

[1] As the writer uses the term "adhesions" here, he means agreements or commitments to support Frederick's position.

honoured as such by the Emperor. On the following day he launched a fresh excommunication against Roland and severe admonitions to the King of Sicily and the Lombards.

The schism had now become incurable. Alexander did not stagger under the blow. He issued an excommunication against Frederick and renewed the ban already laid on Octavian and his party. Thus asserting his authority, he released Frederick's subjects from their obedience, encouraged the Lombards to revolt, and fomented the internal discords of Germany. Meanwhile he maintained his cause throughout the rest of Europe, writing to the bishops at large, and exhorting them to support him among their flocks and before their sovereigns. The support of the episcopate was in fact of great use to him in the various courts of Europe, and especially in those of France and England, two centres of influence of the highest importance. Frederick made vain efforts to gain the kings of these countries; they maintained a prudent reserve, which after some hesitation settled down into an attitude decidedly favourable to Alexander.

The part taken by the Emperor in this struggle for the Papacy did not turn him from his fixed resolve to subdue Lombardy to obedience, and root out all possibility of resistance by bringing Milan to his feet. The calamities and destruction of Crema did not avail to break the spirit of the unyielding Lombard towns opposed to the Emperor, and they rose again in arms, reinvigorated by their alliance with the Pope. In order to assert his sway it was necessary for Frederick to strike a mortal blow at Milan and thus cut out the heart of the Lombard resistance. But it was not an easy undertaking, and all Barbarossa's power might have been shattered but for the assistance of the cities which stood by him faithfully. Their municipal hatred of the great sister city waxed ever stronger as the struggle went on, and caused a wretched denial in the face of the foreigner of those bonds of unselfishness and of blood which ought to have drawn them closely together. With such auxiliaries Frederick began operations against Milan, and for a whole year there was constant warfare in the surrounding territory, with alternating success and a cruel destruction of the great Lombard plain. In the spring of 1161 Germany and Hungary sent the reinforcements necessary for the campaign, and the Emperor was able to shut in the city

more closely. A long siege followed, lasting yet another year.
The defenders held out as long as was possible with unshaken
tenacity, but in the end the forces of resistance failed. The flower
of the garrison had fallen at their posts, disease and hunger were
rapidly cutting off the remnant, munitions of defence had given
out, all resources were exhausted. There was nothing to be done
but to make terms, and all attempts were vain to secure some
favourable agreement previous to surrender. In March 1162 the
vanquished city had to stoop low and submit at the conqueror's
discretion. The sight of the misery and fall of so great and noble
a city aroused pity even in her enemies, who could not refrain
from appealing to the clemency of Frederick. The stern ruler
would not bend, but turned a heart of stone to their prayers.
For him harshness in this case was justice. The imperial majesty
must be vindicated by a signal example of rigour which should
extirpate all hope of future conflict. Milan, given over to pillage
and fire, seemed buried forever beneath the mass of her own ruins.

To those Milanese who survived the siege were assigned four
localities where they might settle, not very far from the ruined
city. It was a grievous dispersion, yet a contemporary chronicler
accused Frederick at a later date of a want of foresight in having
allowed the Milanese to remain so near to the ashes of their
fallen city. But how could it have been possible to imagine a
speedy resurrection after such a fall, and that Milan might rise
again, when Frederick's power had reached such a height and
was inspiring everywhere both reverence and terror? All opposition gave way before him. Piacenza and Brescia had to accept
his stern conditions. Their walls were demolished; the imperial
officials were received; tribute and hostages were rendered to the
Emperor; the imperial Pope was recognised, while the Bishop of
Piacenza, whose loyalty to Alexander was untainted, passed into
exile. Other cities underwent the same ordeal. The imperial
claims asserted at Roncaglia held the field. The dissensions of the
Lombard cities had borne the bitter fruit of misery and servitude,
but a fruit destined in its bitterness to be one of remedy and
healing.

The victories in Lombardy now strengthened Frederick's proj-
ects with regard to Sicily and the East, where the help of maritime
forces was indispensable. He therefore first offered induce-

ments to Pisa and then to Genoa to form an alliance with him. Both consented, although each was distrustful of the other, and Genoa in particular gave adhesion from motives of expediency rather than from any friendly intention. The position in northern Italy being thus secured and a powerful naval connexion being established on the sea, Frederick might well feel assured that within his grasp lay the dominion of all Italy, and that he was on the verge of entering upon the lordship of a genuine and incontestable empire. But Alexander III, despite the grave anxieties of his position, was keeping a watchful eye on this policy with the intention of arresting its achievement. While the war in Lombardy lasted, the Pope, unable to keep a footing in Rome, had remained in the Campagna. In spite of Frederick, all Europe outside the Empire and the Latin East now acknowledged him, but his material resources were such that he was bound to quit Italy and throw himself upon the traditional hospitality of the French kingdom. He embarked at Capo Circello on a galley of the King of Sicily, and after a halt at Genoa entered France through Provence, where he was received everywhere with signs of deep devotion. Well aware of Frederick's commanding influence, he turned to Eberhard of Salzburg, the prelate most loyal to him in Germany, who had brought all his authority to bear on Frederick in order that he might relinquish the schism and make peace with the Church. But the Pope could only put slender trust in these pacific proposals, and within a short month, in 1162, the struggle still continuing, he renewed his excommunications against Octavian and the Emperor in a solemn act of promulgation at Montpellier. In the meantime, Alexander was keeping up his relations with France and England with a view to gaining their decisive adherence to his cause. Nor did he neglect any means of attracting German sympathy and that of Italy, and by raising difficulties in the path of Octavian of dealing a blow at the policy of Frederick. Octavian, in his turn, in two synods held at Lodi and Cremona, had confirmed the decisions of the Council of Pavia, but it was not difficult to see that Alexander's adherents were gaining in number and that Octavian's party was lukewarm and more of a make-believe than a reality. Alexander could only be overcome by shattering his foundations and depriving him of the asylum which was at once his refuge and his strength.

While he appeared to be preparing for an expedition in the South, Frederick turned back and, leaving his representatives in Lombardy charged to keep that province in subjection, he crossed the Alps. Taking advantage of the disputes between England and the French King Louis VII, he turned to the latter in the hope of making him an ally and separating him from the Pope. Louis hesitated; at the instigation of certain councillors who were strongly in favour of an alliance with the Emperor, he began to treat with Frederick and finally with Octavian, while at the same time he made no break in his relations with Alexander, who watched with anxious attention this turn in French policy. It was settled that the two sovereigns should meet on 29 August 1162 at St. Jean-de-Losnes on the frontiers of France and the County of Burgundy, now subject to Frederick. Henry of Champagne, brother-in-law of King Louis, was the soul of these negotiations, and it suited his interests to separate Louis from Henry II of England. The two sovereigns were to bring with them the two pretenders to the Papacy and to arrive together at a final recognition of the true Pope, but if one of the two rivals refused to appear then the other was to be recognised on the spot. Later the king asserted that Henry had gone beyond his instructions in accepting this condition: but meanwhile Alexander, perceiving the serious danger of such an interview, made every effort to prevent its taking place. He was in time to have a conversation with Louis, and if he did not succeed in dissuading him from the meeting he at least was able to convince him that he, the Vicar of Christ, could not bow to the decision of the proposed tribunal. Louis, shaken by the Pope's arguments, made his way to the banks of the Saône in an uncertain mood and anxious to find a means of extricating himself from the complications in which Henry of Champagne had involved him. He was also apprehensive of the show of force with which the Emperor came to meet him, and Frederick himself had his own suspicions. The latter arrived with his own Pope, Victor IV, at the place of meeting, but, not finding the king there, withdrew. Soon afterwards Louis arrived and hearing of the Emperor's withdrawal took his departure without waiting to see if he would return. Thus the interview between the two sovereigns never took place.

Perhaps there was no real wish on either side for the meeting.

But Henry of Champagne in his vexation threatened to transfer his allegiance to the Emperor, and so constrained Louis to promise to return in three weeks in readiness to accept, along with Frederick, the decisions of a congress. This was a mortal blow for Alexander, but he did not lose courage. He brought every kind of influence to bear on Louis, and shewed great political shrewdness in turning to the King of England who was suspicious of an alliance between France and the Emperor, even succeeding in bringing about an understanding between him and the King of France. Thus when Frederick felt most sure of his position he found himself threatened by an unexpected danger, and made up his mind to withdraw from the conference. The Emperor's defection caused no regret to Louis. He returned to Dijon freed from the obligations into which he had entered almost against his will. Before leaving Burgundy, Frederick had held a diet in which Victor IV, while affirming his rights, had excommunicated Alexander III. The latter, in the meanwhile, had enjoyed a triumph at Coucy-sur-Loire. There the Kings of England and of France paid him reverence together and declared him to be the valid and legitimate Pope. In the presence of this triumphant success the anti-Pope's importance was diminished. The struggle between the Papacy and the Empire reverted to great principles and issues, and although the two chief litigants were then at a distance, both appealed to the name of Rome, and the name of Rome once more localised in Italy the arena of combat.

In Italy signs were not wanting that Frederick, notwithstanding the destruction of Milan and the dismantling of the cities in alliance with her, was far from having stamped out all resistance. The heart of the people was unconquerable, and beat in expectation of the hour when they could rise again for the struggle. The affairs of Germany held the Emperor there under weighty responsibilities, while his representatives in Lombardy were imposing cruel exactions on the subject populations. These called in vain for justice. Day by day their yoke became more galling, and if the terrible fate of Milan warned them to endure the burden, still the germs of revolt were ripening below the surface. The Chancellor Rainald of Dassel was indefatigable in checking disaffection and in preparing the naval expedition against Sicily, in the absence of the Emperor, but his adversaries were not idle.

Alexander III, the Kings of Sicily and France, the Emperor of Constantinople, Venice, and the Lombard cities, had come to an agreement among themselves. The forces of resistance were quickened into life. When in October 1163 Frederick with a small army re-entered Lombardy, he was met on all sides by complaints of the rapacity of his agents and by appeals to mitigate the hardships of the oppressed populations. But Frederick gave little heed to such appeals, and the sufferers felt that succour must be sought amongst themselves. Venice gave them encouragement. While the Emperor was engaged in appointing one of his creatures as king in Sardinia without estranging Genoa and Pisa, who were disputing with each other the possession of this island, Verona, Padua, and Vicenza rose in joint rebellion to offer a common resistance and to maintain the rights which ancient custom had handed down. Frederick was suddenly faced by the fact that the league might embrace a wider compass and, being without sufficient force to quell the insurgent communes, he made efforts to pacify them. In this attempt he failed. He therefore sought aid from Pavia, Mantua, and Ferrara, whom he loaded with privileges, trying to move them to hostile action against the League. But the allies appeared in such strong force that he had temporarily to renounce the hazard of battle.

In the meanwhile the anti-Pope Victor had died, in April 1164, at Lucca. The position of Alexander III being thenceforth secure, Frederick might not have been altogether indisposed to renew attempts at reconciliation, but the Archbishop of Cologne, Rainald of Dassel, the implacable enemy of Alexander, stood in his way and obtained the immediate election of another anti-Pope. This was Guido of Crema, who took the name of Paschal III. From the moment of his election the Emperor took him under his protection, and, on his return to Germany, tried to make the German and Italian bishops acknowledge him, but this scheme met with open opposition in the episcopate of both countries. Among the Germans, the Archbishop-elect of Mayence, Conrad of Wittelsbach, rather than yield went into exile in France, near Alexander. The Archbishops of Trèves, Magdeburg, and Salzburg, and the Bishop of Brixen held out, refusing to accept an election so patently uncanonical; while many others of less courage submitted in appearance only to the imperial will.

This opposition, which augmented Frederick's difficulties in Germany, also encouraged the Lombards to shake off their yoke. Alexander III, now that hope of reconciliation with Barbarossa had proved fallacious, was doing all in his power to spur on the resistance of Lombardy, relying on the determination and love of liberty among the communes. Thus by stirring up the cities to rebellion and by devising means for drawing together more closely the adverse powers of Europe, the able policy of Alexander aimed at isolating Frederick and placing him in a position of marked inferiority in his struggle with the Church. The Emperor, wishing to break through the ring of hostile influences which encompassed him, turned to Henry II of England. This monarch was bound to the King of France by very fragile ties, and had deep causes of dissension with the Pope, owing to the struggle which had arisen with Thomas Becket. This dispute was undoubtedly the source of serious difficulties for Alexander III, difficulties which only came to an end on Becket's tragic death. The Emperor and the King of England took advantage of this event to draw closer together, yet without essentially modifying the Pope's position towards Frederick. Alexander was now recognized as the uncontested head of Christendom. He felt strong enough to reoccupy his see and carry on the struggle, which threatened to be renewed with greater tenacity than ever. Through the aid of his vicar, the Cardinal of SS. John and Paul, the Pope had secured guarantees for his safe residence in Rome, and in October 1165 he left France where his reception had been so generous. He travelled to Messina by sea. From Palermo the King of Sicily sent him gifts and ordered an escort of galleys to convey him honourably to Rome, where the Pope made a solemn entry on 23 November. He at once took up his residence in the Lateran. From Germany, whither he had returned and which he was striving to pacify, the Emperor could not fail to perceive that the triumphs of his rival in Rome were a source of dangers which it would be necessary to dispel. He felt that the loyalty of the Lombard cities was no longer to be reckoned upon, and therefore began to recruit an army powerful enough to be confident of success and capable of crushing any resistance from one end of Italy to the other. In order to conjure back more and more the majesty of the Empire, he had Charlemagne canonised by the anti-Pope Paschal III on the Christmas festival of 1165. But times had changed and altered situations had arisen for the Papacy, the Empire, and the peoples now awakened to a new life. Frederick Barbarossa in his lofty aspirations had no conception that he was summoning from the tomb of his great predecessor in Aix-la-Chapelle the phantom of a past for which there was no longer a place amid the living.

19   *Frank Barlow*
          The Feudal Kingdom of England

Profesor Barlow's statement analyzes further the details of the Constitutions of Clarendon, particularly article 3. The writer here shows the rising influence of legal studies, especially Gratian's Decretum. This compilation of church law, called "The Concordance of Discordant Canons," drawn up during the earlier part of the twelfth century, became a basic reference guide for those who supported strong ecclesiastical courts.

Barlow shows the conflict over jurisdiction as Henry's appeal to history and tradition, standing in opposition to the archbishop's appeal to the forceful new studies of ecclesiastical law. He also introduces, as other writers have done, the personal cast of characters, including the archbishop of York, the bishop of London, and John of Salisbury.

By 1162 Henry had become interested in the jurisdiction claimed by the church within his dominions. His father had been a doughty, if unsuccessful, champion of the lay authority in his fiefs; and Henry, although a pious prince, was most jealous of his rights. During Stephen's reign the lack of governance had compelled a willing church to encroach on the half-paralysed secular administration; yet, although the church's power had increased

SOURCE. Frank Barlow, *The Feudal Kingdom of England*, New York: Longmans, Green and Co., 1955, pp. 290–299. Reprinted by permission of Longmans, Green and Co., David McKay Company, Inc.; and the author.

almost as haphazardly as the baronial, its acquisitions lay mainly within a sphere already staked out by its lawyers and militant members and could be regarded more as a tardy and partial satisfaction of outstanding claims than as a usurpation. Even so, the English church moved warily when Henry succeeded to the throne; and under the guidance of the old and prudent Theobald flattered the young man in order to conserve its new position. Henry was no less cautious. Faced with an ageing body of bishops, most of whom had been elected under abnormal conditions, and requiring the moral support of the clergy while he established his rule, he avoided cause for offence and bided his time. But no one expected the peace to last long. Most of the clergy were aware that some regrettable compromises would have to be accepted, some odious wrongs endured; and it was largely with pained resignation that the bishops accepted the promotion of the royal chancellor to the primacy on 27 May 1162, a year after the death of Archbishop Theobald.

The church was still engaged in defining the legitimate interest it allowed the lay government in the appointment to bishoprics. On 5 February 1156 Pope Adrian IV had tightened the regulations by making general Eugenius III's judgment in the William fitz-Herbert case that secular pressure on an electoral body invalidated the election; but, although a twelfth-century prince had to walk with circumspection, Henry could not doubt that once he became strong, chapters would elect his candidates in canonical form. The election of Thomas Becket to Canterbury was Henry's first success. Thomas had served the king well as chancellor, and the king required an archbishop who would serve him just as faithfully. But both Theobald, who had recommended Thomas as his successor, and Henry, who with some hesitation accepted the choice, had miscalculated. Theobald had chosen a man who, he believed, would defend the liberties of the church adroitly while remaining a friend of the king. Henry had selected a man who, he imagined, would help him restore the church to its traditional position. The hopes of both were defrauded. The adroitness with which the humble clerk had risen to such eminence had been an almost intolerable strain on his inclinations and natural character, and he discarded it with relief as soon as he could with safety. As archbishop of Canterbury he needed no longer be all things to all men. He had become a great man in his own right. On 10 August 1162 the archbishop, bare-footed in his cathedral, received the pallium sent by the pope, the livery of his new predecessors and returned the chancellor's seals to the king.

Henry suffered this deception at the very moment when he had started to put his plans into action. With Archbishop Theobald dead and the papacy distracted by schism he foresaw no great hindrance to his policy of depriving the national churches of their novel independence, especially as he could appeal to ancient custom and the undoubted privileges of the pious princes, his ancestors. Henry's main attack was directed against the gains of the ecclesiastical courts, for they touched one of the principal functions of kingship and one of its most profitable rights. Ecclesiastical jurisdiction was generally superior in method to its secular rivals. Canon law was being developed by professional lawyers under the influence of Roman jurisprudence and the discipline of scholastic logic, and it displayed a coherence and a rationality which gave it strong powers of attraction. It was, moreover, easy to bring all manner of cases before the *forum ecclesiasticum*, if the litigants so wished, for most disputes involved broken faith and most crimes were sins. As·the king was determined to improve the procedure in the lay courts he could hope to recover much "civil" jurisdiction from the church without provoking more than professional rivalry. But it was quite otherwise when he expressed dissatisfaction with the way in which the church punished its own offending members, for to trespass on the immunity of the clerical caste, to threaten to lay sacrilegious hands on God's anointed, aroused the passionate fears of an institution which was never confident that it was winning its war against the world, the flesh, and the devil.

In February 1162 at Rouen Henry renewed the canons of the Council of Lillebonne (1080), which had defined the competence of ecclesiastical jurisdiction in Normandy in the Conqueror's day; and in 1163 he ordered his officials in Poitou to stop the abuses of the church courts in connexion with cases of land. Becket, sensitive to the royal attitude, began to increase the severity of his penalties. A clerk convicted of theft was branded, another exiled; and a canon of Lincoln, Philip of Brois, who had insulted a royal justice, was sentenced to a heavy fine and public flogging.

But this policy made matters worse, for Henry considered that the church courts were now usurping royal penalties, and in the case of banishment the charge was true. On 1 October 1163 at Westminster Henry complained to the unsympathetic bishops of the unsatisfactory justice done on criminous clerks in ecclesiastical courts. He was convinced that there had been a change since his grandfather's time, and, after a lively debate, he asked the bishops if they were prepared to observe the customs of the kingdom. No bishop, especially the canonists, could with good conscience agree to be bound by lay custom without reservation, all the more since they were aware that by such an action they would be abandoning hard-won privileges which they believed to be theirs by right. But the king had put his case on a reasonable foundation, for he could pose as the conservative reformer who asked for nothing more than the just rights he should have inherited from his ancestors.

The issue had been joined; and Henry concentrated all his effort on bending the bishops to his will. His affection for Archbishop Thomas had already cooled. He had watched with impatience the archbishop, fresh from recovering royal rights for the king, devote all his talents to the recovery of rights lost by Canterbury; at Woodstock in July 1163, when Henry had proposed to transfer to the exchequer a customary payment from land known as the sheriff's aid, Thomas, who had himself been a sheriff's clerk, had shown his new independence and change of allegiance by the stiffest opposition; and after the council of Westminster Henry abruptly disgraced the archbishop and detached the bishops from his side. In January 1164 at Clarendon, near Salisbury, the king brought matters to a head. Once more he required the bishops to assent to the customs of the kingdom as they had stood in his grandfather's day; and, after some bitter sessions, Archbishop Thomas, aware that the pope counselled moderation, and overwhelmed by threats, took an unconditional oath to conform. The rest of the bishops then with reluctance followed his example. But the customs of England had never been written down. So Henry used his favourite device of the inquest and ordered his court to declare the customs. A record of 16 articles was then produced which, when engrossed as a chirograph, the bishops were required to confirm with their seals. The prelates were dismayed. It was one thing to swear to observe customs which were uncertain and open to varied interpretation and another to confirm in full knowledge practices which no good churchman could honourably approve. The primate recovered his courage and refused; the other bishops, however, bewildered and disillusioned, gave way.

For a time the king put his trust in an insecure pope. But repeated missions to the *curia* failed to obtain papal sanction for the constitutions or the grant in satisfactory form of a papal legation to the archbishop of York. And in the end, Henry deliberately contrived the ruin of the primate by trying him for secular offences in the *curia regis*. At Northampton on 8 October Becket was condemned for failing to perform suit in September when he had been summoned to answer the charge of one of his vassals, John fitz-Gilbert the marshal, that justice had been denied him in the archbishop's honorial court; and for this offence all his movable goods were adjudged to lie at the king's mercy. On 9 October the king began to demand account of various sums of money which had passed through Becket's hands while he had been chancellor. And on 13 October, when Becket appealed to the pope against the bishops, who, he feared, would next pass judgment on him on a criminal charge, the king was presented with the very opportunity he sought, for by appealing to the pope the archbishop contravened the customs of the kingdom as recently recorded by the Clarendon inquest. But the bishops evaded pronouncing judgment on this charge of treason; the lay barons faltered in the task; and the primate pushed his way out of court, and by the morning had fled, secretly and in disguise, to the coast.

Henry's callous and intemperate behaviour had defeated its purpose. The agony of conflicting loyalties, the terror of concealed threats, the strain of following an unreliable and irresponsible leader had racked the English bishops almost beyond endurance and had destroyed the cohesion of what must surely have been the finest episcopal bench in Europe. The archbishop himself had gone defiantly, brokenheartedly, into exile. And the Constitutions remained a royal programme devoid of clerical support and discredited through the measures which the king had used to extort assent.

The Constitutions of Clarendon purport to record the royal

rights in ecclesiastical affairs as they existed before the recent lawlessness. And the truth of the record was never disputed: the question at issue was whether such archaic practices could still be tolerated by the church. Naturally, the more venerable the custom the more likely it was to be obnoxious to the reformers. The church could accept the Norman custom that clerks who held baronies of the king should owe him all the usual feudal services except those irreconcilable with their order; but it could hardly approve those rules of the Conqueror which hindered free appeal and recourse to the pope and which restricted the use of ecclesiastical penalties. And, although the agreement between Pope Paschal, Archbishop Anselm, and King Henry I underlay the procedure described for episcopal elections, even that method was beginning to look outmoded and undesirable to the canonists. The clauses which concerned the competence of the rival courts were more debatable, for in the past church and crown had been more concerned with engaging the help of the other to buttress their threatened authority than with disputing each other's jurisdiction. In the Constitutions the king claimed cases of debt and of disputed advowson, and, of course, maintained that he should supervise the punishment of criminous clerks.

The position of a clerk accused of felony or of a breach of the king's peace (crimes reserved to the king) is described—far too concisely—in article 3 of the Constitutions. Such a clerk is to appear in the royal court when summoned and plead to the charge. If he pleads his clergy the court will consider where he is to stand his trial. If it is decided to hand him over to the bishop so that he may be tried according to canon law a royal officer will go with him to watch the proceedings for the king. Finally, if the accused is found, or pleads, guilty in the ecclesiastical court he is no longer to be protected by the church. It is clear that two separate threats to clerical immunity can be detected in this procedure. In the first place it is recognized that the clerk, when identified as such, may have to face a trial in the royal court itself. The charges to which clerical immunity could not be pleaded are not listed; but it is known that in the Anglo-Norman period, forest offences and treason fell within this category. The second threat is more oblique but more consequential, and it is that which aroused the most opposition. The cryptic conclusion to the clause—that the church was not to protect clerks found guilty of the crimes in question—was generally interpreted as meaning, and was probably intended to secure, that the condemned clerks should be degraded from their sacred orders, rearrested as laymen by the royal officer who had been present at their trial, and taken back to the royal court to receive without further trial the ordinary secular penalty for the crime—usually mutilation or death.

This article 3 of the Constitutions was most offensive to the primate, presumably because it pronounced on the controversy which had provoked the king to hold the inquiry. But Becket could find little in the current text books of canon law on which to base his case. It was certainly illegal to try a clerk on a criminal charge by secular law in a lay court; but Henry infringed this principle only by making exceptions to the rule, and these exceptions were allowed in the final settlement. Moreover, such guidance as the canonists gave on the practice of punishing a degraded clerk by secular penalties favoured the king. In the year 539 the Emperor Justinian had enacted in his 83rd Novel just such a procedure as was declared to be English custom; and, although the canonist Gratian ignored this regulation, he was perfectly familiar with the procedure whereby clerks guilty of heinous clerical offences, such as rebellion against their bishop, were degraded and handed over to the lay power for punishment. Indeed, it would seem that during the preceding centuries the church had taken little interest in the fate of those members it had expelled. Nevertheless, it may be thought that Henry's insistence on the initiative to be taken by the secular power and his intention to use the church courts in this matter simply as instruments for the condemnation and degradation of criminous clerks were out of harmony with the general spirit of the reformed ecclesiastical jurisprudence, and that his plans to establish a royal police system under which clerical criminals should be effectively caught and then suffer almost automatically as laymen was contrary to the policy of the church. What is more, his project did injury to sentiments which, although poorly presented by the canons, were strongly felt. The early church had been prodigal with threats of degradation—and these can be read in the *Decretum*—but the medieval church, under normal conditions and when left to itself, was less severe. To add capital punishment to degradation did violence to its idea of justice, and, since the belief was spreading that Holy Orders were a sacrament and that they left an indelible mark, the too sudden change of character offended its sense of decorum. Archbishop Thomas argued that degradation was a sufficient penalty in itself and that degraded clerks should be punished by the lay power only if they offended again, and used, not unreasonably, Jerome's commentary on Nahum, as employed by the Apostolic Canons and as quoted by Gratian—"Non judicat deus bis in idipsum" (For God does not judge twice for the same offence)—to justify his view. But this argument had its weakness and dangers, for Henry was not advocating a double trial or judgment for a single offence, and the canonists themselves required the prince to add a second penalty in certain cases.

It cannot be doubted that, while the inquisition of January 1164 declared with substantial truth the customs of England, some of those customs were directly opposed to the law of the church and others had become most unpopular. The opponents of the Constitutions did not question their authenticity. Their appeal lay from custom to the law, from history to justice; and Archbishop Thomas in exile based his case upon the book, on the latest codification of canon law, Gratian's *Decretum*, although, as we have seen, that work was not without ambiguity on the subject of criminous clerks. Yet, even if the English customs were at variance with the law of the church as interpreted at the time they could still be tolerated as special custom provided that they were not wrong in themselves. There were always radicals ready to invoke fundamental principle whenever the sphere of ecclesiastical clashed with secular government, and it was not difficult to condemn some of the Anglo-Norman regulations as inherently bad; but in general the Constitutions dealt with matters which were usually treated as political and as subject to diplomatic agreement between the pope and the lay powers. Indeed, the whole juridical controversy was in its nature no more intractable than other disputes, such as that over the investiture of clerks, which had run their courses and been settled by compromise.

In 1164 the situation was envenomed by bitterness and distorted by adventitious elements. Henry pursued the "traitor" archbishop with passionate animosity and refrained from no action, however mean and cruel, which could hurt. Thomas, less powerful and, perhaps, more affected by their old friendship, directed his occasional rash acts of severity against the "traitor" bishops and archdeacons. None of the principal parties, however, wanted the quarrel to get completely out of hand, and the violent expressions of a violent age (so voluminously preserved) to some extent obscure the patient negotiation between king, pope, and archbishop, which continued almost without interruption. Although no English bishop was uncritically loyal to the king—and men so deeply influenced by canon law and new spirit in the church could not be expected blindly to follow a lay prince in such a cause—none was prepared to enlist under the doubtful banner of the archbishop. Thomas's promotion had disappointed the ambition of some and outraged the sense of propriety of others. His intimacy with the king in the past made his motives suspect and his tactlessness unforgivable, while his ostentation both as courtier and as archbishop stamped him as a parvenu; so that his championship of the common cause made the case itself appear less honest. And these taints, which no extreme of asceticism, no discipline in the new life could wash away, deprived him of that integrity, that natural holiness, and that moral authority which illuminate a saint in his lifetime and which Anselm had so conspicuously displayed. It was an act of murder which made Thomas a saint, and even his passion was smirched by a foul word.

No one hated Thomas more than another who might have become a saint and an archbishop, Gilbert Foliot, sometime prior of Cluny, prior of Abbeville, abbot of Gloucester, bishop of Hereford (1148), and, since 1163, bishop of London, a man of noble birth, and able governor, and a famous ascetic, and one who could not forgive Thomas because he was the wrong man championing the cause of right. For the archbishop of York, Roger of Pont-l'Évêque, Canterbury's disgrace was York's opportunity. There had been enmity between the two men in Archbishop Theobald's household—Roger who became archdeacon of Canterbury in 1148, resenting Thomas's climb to importance through the old archbishop's doting favour—and, when Thomas fell, Roger aspired to keep and to extend the privileges he had acquired for his metropolitan see while the southern province had lacked a pastor. This personal struggle, clothed now in constitutional garb, was perhaps, the bitterest ingredient in the whole conflict. Chichester and Salisbury, too, were opposed to Becket. Others vacillated or shut their eyes. Worcester went abroad to study. Only the aged Henry of Winchester, secure in his rank and his fame, dared, quietly but consistently, to take the exile's side.

The judge to whom all the disputants looked, Pope Alexander III, a Sienese, was the finest canonist and theologian of them all. His *Summa*, known as the *Stroma*, one of the earliest commentaries on Gratian, and his *Sententiae*, a theological exercise influenced by Abalard, had adorned his teaching career at Bologna; and his work as papal chancellor had given him a clear understanding of the working of the papal government. Indebted to Henry for his recognition and threatened by a rival under the patronage of the Emperor Frederick I, Alexander showed himself to be a statesman with the true Italian touch. Although Becket's stand was inopportune and his behaviour often an embarrassment, the pope never let the archbishop down, and his diplomatic finesse was such that neither was Thomas completely disheartened nor was Henry entirely unhopeful during the seven years the quarrel lasted. Alexander, in exile at Sens, did not hesitate to confirm immediately the archbishop's condemnation of certain of the Constitutions. Obnoxious chapters were those which restricted the right of appeal and of exit from England and the freedom to punish and coerce the king's tenants-in-chief and servants by sentences of excommunication and interdict, that which restored to the royal court disputes over the advowson of churches, and, of course, the clause concerning criminous clerks. Other chapters were anathematized as the quarrel developed, until about half of these English customs came under the ban. But the pope, prudent and conciliatory both by nature and training, was not prepared to take offensive action; and Becket retired with a few devoted companions to the Cistercian abbey of Pontigny, near Auxerre in Burgundy, where he devoted himself to the study of the *Decretum* and the prosecution of his case, while striving through austerity to prepare himself morally for the lonely path he had chosen.

A fallen upstart has few friends. One, however, Thomas kept, and one worth a thousand: John of Salisbury, the famous author

of the *Policraticus* and *Metalogicon,* both of which works he had
dedicated to Becket, a man familiar with the papal court and
skilled in diplomacy and the composition of persuasive letters.
But in general the beneficed members of the church, while pro-
fessionally sympathetic, were unwilling to risk much for the
exile's cause. Nevertheless, a fire was lit which has never since
been put out. The poor and oppressed, those who groaned under
the weight of the world and suffered under Angevin rule, took
the archbishop to their hearts. For them he became a symbol of
revolt, until legend made him an Englishman resisting the foreign
yoke; and this feeling ensured his sanctity when at last he had
been struck down by the servants of the tyrant, and made possible
the many miracles at his tomb.

20   *Austin Lane Poole*
From Domesday Book to Magna Carta

Writing in the Oxford History *of England,* Professor Austin Lane
Poole *suggests that Becket had little support at home and that he
behaved in a "querulous and acrimonious" manner. Within England
"he seems to have been little missed." He calls attention to "Becket's
violence" rather than the king's.*

*This view clearly contradicts the traditional image of masses of
supporters turning out to greet their popular, long-exiled archbishop
when he returned after a long absence that had left them sorely
bereft.*

In England Becket's flight created little excitement. The usual
measures were taken: an embassy of bishops and barons was dispatched to lay the king's case before the pope at Sens, and the

SOURCE. Austin Lane Poole, *From Domesday Book to Magna Carta,
1087–1216,* Vol. II of *The Oxford History of England,* Oxford: The
Clarendon Press, 1951, 2nd ed. 1955, pp. 209–211. Reprinted by permission
of the publisher.

revenues of the see of Canterbury were confiscated. Henry's vindictiveness in banishing from the country or thrusting into prison the archbishop's relatives and friends was naturally condemned, but otherwise his actions at this time seem to have met with the general approval of both laymen and churchmen. William of Newburgh, a man of sound common sense, gives it as his personal opinion that the archbishop's conduct could not be regarded as praiseworthy, however much it might have proceeded from a laudable zeal, since it served no useful purpose and only tended further to incense the king. Becket in fact found few sympathizers in England; and it is significant that his prolonged absence abroad seems to have made no difference in the working of the government. In spite of the position which he had occupied in previous years, he seems to have been little missed.

Abroad the affair took on an international aspect. The leading powers sought to make political capital out of it. Louis VII, already the protector of Pope Alexander, became now the protector of Becket, for he had much to gain from the embarrassing position in which his formidable Angevin antagonist was placed in consequence of the archbishop's flight. But, while taking what political advantage he could from the situation, he at the same time made continual and genuine attempts to heal the quarrel. In the course of the six years of 1165–70 he arranged with Henry no less than twelve interviews, ten of which actually took place, where reconciliation of the king and the archbishop was, if not the only, at least a prominent subject of discussion. The emperor for his part saw in the circumstances a possible opportunity of detaching Henry from the side of the legitimate pope. It was dread of this happening that prevented Alexander from adopting a more decisive policy; and even the king of France admitted to John of Salisbury that for this reason he could not undertake to urge the pope to stronger measures. Their fears, indeed, were far from groundless. More than once Henry was on the brink of deserting the pope: at the diet of Würzburg (June 1165), for example, his envoys—whether in obedience to instructions is not clear and their action was afterwards repudiated—pledged their master's allegiance to the anti-pope, Paschal III; and in the following spring Henry wrote in a moment of irritation to the imperial chancellor that he had been long seeking a good excuse for withdrawing his support from Pope Alexander and his treacherous cardinals. But it never came quite to this, for Alexander wisely so tempered his acts as to avoid giving unnecessary offence. Thus when he authorized Becket to use ecclesiastical censures against those who invaded the property of his church, he expressly exempted the king, and when a little later (April 1166) he bestowed on Becket a legatine commission throughout England, he excepted the diocese of York. Nevertheless, the situation was involved and intricate, and much depended on the diplomatic tact with which it was handled.

Although Henry was himself a good diplomat, he had in former years entrusted delicate business of this sort to his chancellor, Becket, who managed it with supreme success. Now that Becket's services were no longer at his disposal, he had to rely on men of less commanding personality. However, the men who formed his *corps diplomatique* during the critical years from 1164 to 1170 were shrewd and able politicians, whose significance may be judged from the bitter invective levelled against them by the archbishop and his partisans. John of Oxford, afterwards bishop of Norwich, Richard of Ilchester, archdeacon of Poitiers and later bishop of Winchester, both royal judges, and John Cumin, who ended a strenuous life in the king's service as archbishop of Dublin, were the most prominent among Henry's ambassadors. It was they who were sent on diplomatic missions to Rome, to the imperial court, and to France, they that carried through the complicated intrigues to which Becket's exile on the Continent gave rise.

We need not dwell on the tedious details of the long struggle. Becket in his refuge in the Cistercian abbey of Pontigny employed his time in study and in conducting a voluminous correspondence with his friends and enemies. While seeking to justify his own conduct, he dilated upon his supposed injuries. The tone of his letters became more and more querulous and acrimonious, rising in crescendo till it reached a climax with the famous missives in which he announced the sentences of excommunication delivered at Vézelay against his adversaries. Richard de Lucy, the justiciar, and Jocelin of Balliol as the prime authors of the Constitutions of Clarendon, were especially singled out, but all who had observed or supported them were included in the condemnation; John of

Oxford and Richard of Ilchester were excommunicated for having had dealings with the schismatic pope, and Rannulf de Broc and others for having "usurped" the possessions of the see of Canterbury. Even the king himself was threatened with similar treatment. The bishops remonstrated and appealed to the pope, while the king retaliated by bringing pressure to bear on the Cistercian order to obtain the archbishop's removal from Pontigny. But it was again the political situation which saved Henry from the effects of Becket's violence; for the pope, hard pressed in the autumn of 1166 by the emperor's invading armies, could ill afford to increase the number of his enemies. He therefore annulled the sentences passed by Becket, inhibited him for the time being from further molesting the king, and appointed legates, one of whom—William of Pavia—was prejudiced against Becket, even, in fact, his avowed enemy, to arbitrate in the quarrel (December 1166). The cardinals proceeded with their task in the dilatory way commonly followed by papal legates, and the whole of the year 1167 was frittered away without anything being accomplished. The archbishop was prepared to agree to any and every proposal, but with the exasperating evasive qualification *salvo honore Dei* and *salvo ordine suo*. It was insistence on these formulae which wrecked the chances of a reconciliation when the two opponents met for the first time since their quarrel on 6 January 1169 at Montmirail in Maine. Becket's best friends, even the clerks who shared his exile, urged him to omit the offending words; but in vain, and a great opportunity for peace was lost. Another conference held in the autumn at Montmartre outside Paris miscarried on a point no less trivial: all was going smoothly, everything of importance had been conceded, but Henry refused to ratify the compact by giving Becket the kiss of peace.

21   *Amy Kelly*
Eleanor of Aquitaine

The central figure in Professor Amy Kelly's delightful biography is neither the king of England nor the archbishop of Canterbury, but Eleanor, the royal spouse who left the bed of King Louis VII to transfer her person and her extensive lands to Henry. Although the queen was not directly involved with Becket's troubles, Professor Kelly deals here with the archbishop's attempt to undercut royal support by excommunicating those who most actively sided with the king; she describes Henry's countermoves in dramatic detail. Alexander III, once again seen as a central figure, was forced by the pressures of both sides to employ the most skillful sort of diplomacy. Reference to Alexander's letters to Thomas and to Count Ugo Balzani's article will help to balance this account of the papal role in the controversy.

Becket, after his first successes in the *curia* and the French court, was persuaded by his friends to give up his episcopal retinue and bide the issue of a struggle that must be protracted, in some retirement, where maintenance of his dignities would be less expensive to those who were supporting not only his exile, but the banishment of all his kin. These friends hinted that a cloistral seclusion might, in the circumstances, do more for the stakes at issue than any insistence on those temporal grandeurs to which Thomas was accustomed. Becket willingly submitted his person to the hair shirt and cowl, the regimen of fasts and vigils; but when he put on the white wool cassock of the Cistercians blessed for his use by Alexander and retired to the simiplicity of the abbey of Pontigny, it was not to a mystical retreat. He busied himself collecting works on the canon law and worked up his

SOURCE. Amy Kelly, *Eleanor of Aquitaine and the Four Kings*, Cambridge, Mass.: Harvard University Press. Copyright, 1950, by the President and Fellows of Harvard College, pp. 128–133. Reprinted by permission of the publishers.

case, item by item. He beset his suffragans, the chapters of the orders, the courts and chancelleries of Europe, and the *curia* with a tide of correspondence, brief upon brief, arguing his position, insisting upon his salvos, inveighing against the "constitutions," pressing for the redress of his grievances, which were the grievances of Rome.

Early in 1166 Alexander's own prospects against the antipope and the Holy Roman Emperor brightened for a season, and he was able to return for an interval to Rome. In this auspicious moment he raised Becket's fortunes with his own. At Easter he made the exiled archbishop legate for all England save the diocese of York, which had anciently been excluded from the governance of Canterbury. Thus, even though Henry's malice thwarted Thomas from the exercise of his authority as primate, he might use his legatine authority from abroad to control his rebellious bishops in England and to threaten the king. Armed with these extraordinary powers, Becket sought to force from Henry the surrender of his sequestered see.

Henry and Eleanor were holding their Easter court in Angers when this alarming edict went forth from Rome. Very expeditiously, on the Sunday following, three of Becket's closest friends arrived at Angers with demands for the restoration of the properties of Canterbury and the repatriation of the exiles. Henry received them superciliously and sent them back to Pontigny with dry evasive answers and the veiled threat that, if he were pressed by papal legates in his affairs with his primate, he would seek his safety with the schismatic German emperor. He had already been dangling this sword above the papal conclaves by threatening to affiance his eldest daughter Matilda to the nephew of the emperor.

When his envoys returned to Pontigny empty handed, Becket addressed three successive letters to the king, which were marked by a sharp crescendo. They passed swiftly from pastoral admonition to condign threats. First, he reminded Henry that, as his spiritual father, he was above all mindful of his spiritual weal, and that, after Henry had submitted himself to correction, he would find Thomas's grace to him unbounded; next, he reminded the king that sovereigns receive their glaive from the church and warned him lest his arrogance lead him to error and perdition;

and finally, having had no answer to these admonitions, he served notice that, if the king did not shortly change his evil courses, something a good deal more dire than warnings would swiftly follow. He concluded this correspondence by giving Henry the term until Pentecost for penance and reflection.

Nothing was more ineffectual with Henry than unction. The warning letters did not produce the expected collapse in Angers. Henry remarked to his entourage that in his previous experience with Becket he had often known the archbishop to mistake his own will for that of Providence. The king did, however, take measures to defend himself. Although he had decreed in the Constitutions of Clarendon that appeals to Rome should be unlawful, he himself sent off an embassy to Alexander demanding restraint of the intolerable Thomas; and in the meantime, as a practical rejoinder to Becket, he dispatched to the abbé of the Cistercians, then in chapter, a threat to confiscate all the Cistercian properties in England unless the order ceased at once to harbor Becket and his fellow exiles in their house of Pontigny.

Henry's bold gestures could not, however, conceal the fact that anathema, possibly interdict, was again in the air. The Plantagenets would, as a practical matter, dread the effects of fulmination, but more as a political inconvenience than as an actual instrument of damnation. They were less sensitive in this regard than the Capets. The Angevins throughout their generations had now and then been exposed to the censures of the church; and Eleanor, both as heiress of Poitou and as Queen of France, had more than once weathered anathema.

However, anathema and interdict imposed considerable affliction on feudal magnates and alienated the pious common folk from their overlords. Simple souls abhorred as the plague the awful withholding of the sacraments, the darkening of altars, the silencing of the parish bells, the sudden extinction of those communal rites that marked with solemnity and grandeur the narrow round of their existence. The people could not, like powerful nobles, avoid the effect of anathema and interdict. Kings could, of course, as a last resort, protect themselves by threats of schism. They could support antipopes, who could also fulminate, bind and unbind, loose and unloose. But the people had no such resource.

Though the Plantagenets could not be intimidated by any personal dread of interdict, they had at this time a very special reason for not courting a breach with Rome that might make them unpopular throughout their provinces. This reason was the fact that Henry, the heir of England, though now in his twelfth year, had not yet been ceremoniously crowned, consecrated, and recognized by the assembled barons and prelates of Britain as the successor of the conquerors. The custom of anointing the heirs of kings in the lifetime of their sires had been established in Europe. Louis Capet had been consecrated by the Pope himself in the royal cathedral of Reims before the death of Louis the Fat. The birth of the heir of the Capets, diminishing as it did the status of Henry's son in the French court, gave added urgency to the Plantagenet's desire to see the youth firmly established in his English heritage. He had always taken every precaution to secure the recognition of his heir in England; but that actual anointing of the prince had not taken place, and the only person authorized by custom and tradition to consecrate the heir in England was the Archbishop of Canterbury. With his legatine commission from the Pope, Becket was now in a position to prevent any other bishop's serving under an arbitrary mandate from Henry to officiate in his place. It was thus important for the Plantagenets to avoid proceeding to extremity with Rome until the prince should have been established with the indispensable sanctions of the church.

Having flouted Becket's legatine mission in Angers, Henry shut himself up from the world in his fortress castle of Chinon to gain a respite of time. Sick kings were not subject to excommunication, and the chronicle says that Henry was sick in his stronghold above the Vienne. While the king wrestled with his malady, Becket was not idle. He came forth from his Lenten retreat and fortified himself at the shrine of Saint Drausius, the crusader's champion. The spring season for pilgrimage was on, and the people of Champagne and Burgundy, the burghers and scholars of Paris, were on the road. It had gone abroad that Thomas, armed with papal authority, had threatened the King of the English, and that, exiled now from his poor monk's portion in Pontigny by the malice of that king, he was on his way to the great shrine of Saint Mary Magdalene in Vézelay for the day of

Pentecost. The time assigned for Henry's penance had expired. As in the spring of Saint Bernard's condemnation of Abélard at Sens, the people now thronged to a great shrine of Burgundy anticipating another thunderous episode in that everlasting magnificent drama between the powers of light and the powers of darkness.

The vast Cluniac church of Vézelay was that which Abbé Bernard (now named for sainthood) had found too small for his call to the second crusade. It was the center of convocation from whose portals news took wing over the thoroughfares of pilgrimage to the farthest corners of Gaul. On a Sunday of May, before a concourse of "divers nations" and certain distinguished prelates of France, the exiled archbishop, *miser et miserabilis*, but mighty with authority, preached the sermon of Pentecost.

The ritual of excommunication was by custom performed in the narthex, beyond the holy bounds of sanctuary. After the offices, the throngs moved from the nave into the open with a solemn procession of the clergy. There in the entry of the church, the candles were lighted, one for each impenitent; then as the formula was recited, these were extinguished one by one and trampled underfoot; the book was closed; the doors to the sanctuary were barred to those cut off from the church's grace; and bells announce to the whole believing world the expulsion of the excommunicates; their names were fixed to the portals to warn all men, as they loved their own salvation, to shun them. So it was at Vézelay.

After the sermon, Thomas recited the wrongs of the church, reviewed his citation of all the malefactors in service of the king to acknowledgment of their crimes and to repentance, described their stubborn disobedience. When he spoke of his old friend the king, his voice broke and his words were dissolved in tears. But the burden of duty and conscience lay upon him. Denouncing each in turn, and specifying again the sin of each, he did with book, bell, and candle excommunicate Henry's clerks, Richard of Ilchester and John of Oxford for their damnable traffic with schismatics in Germany; Henry's legists, Richard of Lucy and John of Balliol, for setting up the subversive Constitutions of Clarendon; Henry's officers, Ranulf de Broc, Hugh of Saint Clare and Thomas Fitz-Stephen, for their unlawful seizure and holding of properties of Canterbury. No bolt of anathema touched the king directly, but the finger of the archbishop pointed straight at his forehead with a dreadful warning. The Primate of England, armed by the Pope with legatine power, outlawed all the noxious acts of the king's agents and rendered them null and void. Like a ripple widening in a poll, the tidings spread in every direction from Vézelay.

"Rumor does in truth fly on wings to kings and princes," says Hoveden. It was presently said that Henry received the news in Chinon with tears of rage. But when he at last emerged from seclusion he had recovered both health and composure. "As with the voice of a crier" he announced to an astonished world that he had not only the Archbishop of Canterbury but the Pope and the Roman cardinals "in his purse." He related to his familiars how much this business of his had cost in the *curia*. He displayed documents certifying that Alexander, waiving the legateship of Thomas, had given a dispensation to the Archbishop of York to crown the heir of England. He declared that the Pope considered relieving him of his insufferable archbishop by translating Becket to some distant see, perhaps to Sicily. It was rumored that he had offered his infant daughter Joanna to the Prince of Sicily to prosper this arrangement. He gave it out that the censures pronounced by Becket at Vézelay were suspended pending the arrival of papal envoys. Alexander, he proclaimed, was sending two cardinal legates to Gaul to put an end to the intolerable *demarches* of the archbishop against the dignity of the king. These cardinals were William of Pavia and Otto of Ostia, and they were already getting over the Alps. The person who brought these heartening tidings to Chinon was no other than John of Oxford, whom Becket had recently excommunicated at Vézelay, now absolved by agency of the Pope himself.

No one was more dumfounded by this surprising turn of affairs than the Archbishop of Canterbury. William of Pavia was one of his dearest enemies and was now rumored to be Henry's candidate for his see. Otto of Ostia was one to blow neither hot nor cold upon his grievances. Becket's friend, John of Salisbury, familiar with the *curia*, dreaded them both merely as Romans and cardinals. Becket at once surmised that Rome had "smelled of English sterling." He had a vision in which he was offered a cup of poisoned wine from the edges of which two spiders crawled.

The fact was that Alexander was again "in shipwreck," this time in the very trough of the wave. The Holy Roman Emperor's army, abetted, as some suspected, by English subsidy, was at the gates of Rome. In this crisis of his affairs, the Pope wrote to Becket obscurely. "If," he said, "matters do not come off for the moment to your satisfaction, wait for a more favorable time." But patience was not Thomas's most conspicuous virtue. He dipped his pen in gall and composed letters to Alexander and expostulations to the legates, some of which his tactful friend edited and re-edited before they could be dispatched to the Holy See. John observes that in some instances Becket's original language was "not fit to be addressed to the Pope's postilion."

The legates, arrived in Gaul after unexpected delays, found it more difficult than they had imagined to bring the wounded Becket before a tribunal procured in Rome by his adversary. He demurred; he made legal difficulties; he begged the question, declaring he would come to the parley only after the restoration of his see. At last, late in the fall of 1168 (Saint Martin's) he was induced to meet the cardinals at Gisors. Though the legates engaged him cautiously and forbode to press him, they could not bring him to negotiate, nor could they contrive any formula to which he would assent. William and Otto were obliged to retire empty handed to Henry in Argentan. Henry, who had been willing to spend liberally to gain his ends, suffered an attack of Angevin fury at the failure of his mission. The legates were dismissed so promptly, says Diceto, that they did not wait for their own equipage to be assembled, but rode hurriedly away on such horses as they could find, their ears burning with Henry's parting shout, "I hope I may never lay eyes on a cardinal again."

PART FIVE

Three Playwrights View Thomas Becket

THREE PLAYWRIGHTS VIEW
THOMAS BECKET

INTRODUCTION

The body of knowledge about the past that any given person carries with him at a particular point in time, sometimes accurate but always modified by his own experience and insights, is not necessarily handed to him through the craft of the professional historian. Legends, hearsay, faulty memory, prejudice, and the sifted or garbled reports of the novelist, the dramatist, and the poet all contribute to our accumulated impressions of past events.

Thomas Becket and Henry II have been the subjects (or victims) of more fictionalized accounts than most historical figures, perhaps because their institutional roles were so interwoven with their personal existences. In the past few years two widely popular films have dealt with Henry, and various historical novels have been written about Becket.

This section presents short excerpts from three plays of different time periods, each dealing with Becket in a completely different manner. The first is from an obscure drama of the late seventeenth century, probably but not definitely written by Will Mountfort. John Dryden contributed a hackneyed prologue that would not rate as a major contribution to literature. The short scene that follows shows three of Henry's courtiers discussing the Becket affair after the archbishop's death. Referring to him as a "Patron of Rebellion" and a "Traytor to the King and all his Int'rest," they attack the whole clergy in a manner that probably appealed to the Restoration audience.

The second, a short scene from T. S. Eliot's verse play "Murder in the Cathedral," depicts the chorus of Canterbury women in their lament to the archbishop, hero of the downtrodden. Whether the historic Becket was indeed such a hero is at least questionable, but legends of his enormous popularity began to spread right after his death.

Jean Anouilh's "Becket," a great success both on stage and screen, presents a very different Thomas. The scene from the close of Act I shows him, while still chancellor and intimate friend of the king, as a Saxon who wormed his way to the confidence of Henry, the Norman and Angevin, by pimping, fighting, and carousing. Although it is reasonably well established that Becket preserved his chastity (who can say, after all?), Anouilh uses dramatic license to show an established mistress whom Becket betrays.

22   *Will Mountfort and John Bancroft*
"Henry the Second"

SELECTIONS FROM ACT I, SCENE 1

VERULAM: I have observ'd the Crowd of fawning Wretches,
Which servilely attend the Queen's Appartment,
Watching the early op'ning of the Door,
To shew their Zeal.

SUSSEX: The Fathers and the Priests, you mean.

VERULAM: You hit me right.
These holy, pious, seeming godly Men,
Swarm not for nothing: Either there's Revenge
Or Int'rest stirring, when Church-men's diligence
Haunt majesty so much.
I have observ'd how grossly they have flatter'd,
Yet she hath swallow'd up their nauseous Phrases
Fast, as their utt'rance, while they prais'd her Person,
Or loaded with Hyperbole her Son.

SOURCE. A play, "Henry the Second, King of England," attributed to John Bancroft, and Will Mountfort, with a prologue written by John Dryden, written and first performed in 1693.

AUMERLE: You speak of what is natural to Women.

VERULAM: But when they gain'd attention, and wrought her
To admiration, then the Vane was turn'd,
And their foul Breath pointed against the King.
Then Becket's Death, that Patron of Rebellion,
That Traytor to the King and all his Int'rest,
Was introduc'd; and with such doleful Accents,
As if the Life o' th' church expir'd in His.
Here Henry was forgot, her Lord and Monarch;
Instead of punishing the sawcy Gown-man,
She mourn'd the Fall of the aspiring Prelate;
Would cast her Eyes, almost eclips'd with Tears,
On the young Race of Heroes standing by,
Insinuating their Father was too Guilty.

SUSSEX: Nay, they are always ripe for Mischief,
Whene'er the Power o' th' Crown checks that o' th'
Church;
And the World knows too well, if they had Power.

VERULAM: If they had Power! Why have they not, my Lord?
Divide the Globe, and you will find a Third
Are Men in Orders, or the Slaves to them.
I tell you, Sirs, they are a dreadful Host;
And should the Pulpit sound to an Alarm,
I question much whether our Hercules
Could cope this Hydra. 'Tis a horrid Tale
They have possess'd th' unthinking Crowd withal,
Concerning Becket's Death.

AUMERLE: Wou'd the whole Tribe had met the Traytor's Fate,
Since they aspire to fetter Monarchy,
Nay the Nobility must sink with him.

SUSSEX: Whils't ev'ry Pendant which can gain the Rocket
Must Lord it o'er us, we shall be like Beasts
Pegg'd on the Common, there to graze our Round,
And must be thankful, though the Soyl's our own.

AUMERLE: Surely at the last the Royal Soul will rouze
And free himself and People from Yoke.
Oh how I covet such a Jubilee!

VERULAM: I find we centre in Opinion, and shall be
Glad to joyn in such a Cause.—
W'are interrupted, the Court breaks in upon us.

23   *T. S. Eliot*
"Murder in the Cathedral"

CHORUS

We have not been happy, my Lord, we have not been happy.
We are not ignorant women, we know what we must expect
    and not expect.
We know of oppression and torture,
We know of extortion and violence,
Destitution, disease,
The old without fire in winter,
The child without milk in summer,
Our labour taken away from us.
We have seen the young man mutilated,
The torn girl trembling by the mill-stream.
And meanwhile we have gone on living,
Living and partly living,
Picking together the pieces,
Gathering faggots at nightfall,
Building a partial shelter,
For sleeping, and eating and drinking and laughter.
God gave us always some reason, some hope; but now a new
    terror has soiled us, which none can avert, none can avoid,
    flowing under our feet and over the sky;
Under doors and down chimneys, flowing in at the ear and
    the mouth and the eye.

SOURCE. T. S. Eliot, *Murder in the Cathedral.* Copyright, 1935, by Harcourt, Brace & World, Inc.; copyright, 1963, by T. S. Eliot, pp. 42–45. Reprinted by permission of the publisher.

God is leaving us, God is leaving us, more pang, more pain,
  than birth or death.
Sweet and cloying through the dark air.
Falls the stifling scent of despair;
The forms take shape in the air:
Puss-purr of leopard, footfall of padding bear,
Palm-pat of nodding ape, square hyaena waiting
For laughter, laughter, laughter. The Lords of Hell are here.
They curl round you, lie at your feet, swing and wing through
  the dark air.
O Thomas Archbishop, save us, save us, save yourself that we
  may be saved;
Destroy yourself and we are destroyed.

THOMAS

Now is my way clear, now is the meaning plain:
Temptation shall not come in this kind again.
The last temptation is the greatest treason:
To do the right deed for the wrong reason.
The natural vigour in the venial sin
Is the way in which our lives begin.
Thirty years ago, I searched all the ways
That lead to pleasure, advancement and praise.
Delight in sense, in learning and in thought,
Music and philosophy, curiosity,
The purple bullfinch in the lilac tree,
The tiltyard skill, the strategy of chess,
Love in the garden, singing to the instrument,
Were all things equally desirable.
Ambition comes when early force is spent
And when we find no longer all things possible.
Ambition comes behind and unobservable.
Sin grows with doing good. When I imposed the King's law
In England, and waged war with him against Toulouse,
I beat the barons at their own game. I
Could then despise the men who thought me most contemptible,
The raw nobility, whose manners matched their finger nails.
While I ate out of the King's dish

To become servant of God was never my wish.
Servant of God has chance of greater sin
And sorrow, than the man who serves a king.
For those who serve the greater cause may make the cause
  serve them,
Still doing right: and stiving with political men
May make that cause political, not by what they do
But by what they are. I know
What yet remains to show you of my history
Will seem to most of you at best futility,
Senseless self-slaughter of a lunatic,
Arrogant passion of a fanatic.
I know that history at all times draws
The strangest consequence from remotest cause.
But for every evil, every sacrilege,
Crime, wrong, oppression and the axe's edge,
Indifference, exploitation, you, and you,
And you, must all be punished. So must you.
I shall no longer act or suffer, to the sword's end.
Now my good Angel, whom God appoints
To be my guardian, hover over the swords' points.

24   *Jean Anouilh* *"Becket"*

(The KING has moved over to the BARONS who are now snoring on their stools. He gives them a kick as he passes.)

KING: They've fallen asleep, the hogs. That's their way of showing their finer feelings. You know, my little Saxon, sometimes I have the impression that you and I are the only sensitive men in England. We eat with forks and

SOURCE. Jean Anouilh, *Becket of the Honor of God*, translated by Lucienne Hill, pp. 41–47. Copyright 1960 by Jean Anouilh and Lucienne Hill. Reprinted by permission of Coward-McCann, Inc. and Dr. Jan van Loewen Ltd.

we have infinitely distinguished sentiments, you and I. You've made a different man of me, in a way . . . What you ought to find me now, if you loved me, is a girl to give me a little polish. I've had enough of whores. (He has come back to GWENDOLEN. He caresses her a little and then says suddenly) Favor for favor—do you remember? (A pause.)

BECKET: (Pale) I am your servant, my prince, and all I have is yours. But you were gracious enough to say I was your friend.

KING: That's what I mean! As one friend to another it's the thing to do! (A short pause. He smiles maliciously, and goes on caressing GWENDOLEN, who cowers, terrified.) You care about her then? Can you care for something? Go on, tell me, tell me if you care about her? (Becket says nothing. The KING smiles.) You can't tell a lie. I know you. Not because you're afraid of lies—I think you must be the only man I know who isn't afraid of anything—not even Heaven—but because it's distasteful to you. You consider it inelegant. What looks like morality in you is nothing more than esthetics. Is that true or isn't it?

BECKET: (Meeting his eyes, says softly) It's true, my Lord.

KING: I'm not cheating if I ask for her, am I? I said "favor for favor" and I asked you for your word of honor.

BECKET: (Icily) And I gave it to you.

(A pause. They stand quite still. The KING looks at BECKET with a wicked smile. BECKET does not look at him. Then the KING moves briskly away.)

KING: Right. I'm off to bed. I feel like an early night tonight. Delightful evening, Becket. You're the only man in England who knows how to give your friends a royal welcome. (He kicks the slumbering BARONS.) Call my guards and help me wake these porkers. (The BARONS wake with sights and belches as the KING pushes them about, shouting:) Come on, Barons, home! I know you're connoisseurs of good music, but we can't listen to music all night long. Happy evenings end in bed, eh Becket?

BECKET: (Stiffly) May I ask your Highness for a brief moment's grace?

KING: Granted! Granted! I'm not a savage. I'll wait for you both in my litter. You can say good night to me downstairs.

(He goes out, followed by the BARONS. BECKET stands motionless for a while under GWENDOLEN'S steady gaze. Then he says quietly:)

BECKET: You will have to go with him, Gwendolen.

GWENDOLEN: (Composedly) Did my Lord promise me to him?

BECKET: I gave him my word as a gentleman that I would give him anything he asked for. I never thought it would be you.

GWENDOLEN: If he sends me away tomorrow, will my lord take me back?

BECKET: No.

GWENDOLEN: Shall I tell the girls to put my dresses in the coffer?

BECKET: He'll send over for it tomorrow. Go down. One doesn't keep the king waiting. Tell him I wish him a respectful good night.

GWENDOLEN: (Laying her viol on the bed) I shall leave my Lord my viol. He can almost play it now. (She asks, quite naturally) My Lord cares for nothing in the whole world, does he?

BECKET: No.

GWENDOLEN: (Moves to him and says gently) You belong to a conquered race too. But through tasting too much of the honey of life, you've forgotten that even those who have been robbed of everything have one thing left to call their own.

BECKET: (Inscruptably) Yes, I daresay I had forgotten. There is a gap in me where honor ought to be. Go now.

(GWENDOLEN goes out. BECKET stands quite still. Then he goes to the bed, picks up the viol, looks at it, then throws it abruptly away. He pulls

off the fur coverlet and starts to unbutton his
doublet. A GUARD comes in, dragging the SAX-
ON GIRL from the forest, whom he throws down
in the middle of the room. The KING appears.)

KING: (Hilariously) Thomas, my son! You'd forgotten her!
You see how careless you are! Luckily I think of everything. It seems they had to bully the father and the
brother a tiny bit to get her, but anyway, here she is.
You see?—I really am a friend to you, and you're wrong
not to love me. You told me you fancied her. I hadn't
forgotten that, you see. Sleep well, son.

(He goes out, followed by the GUARD. The
GIRL, still dazed, looks at BECKET who has not
moved. She recognizes him, gets to her feet and
smiles at him. A long pause, then she asks with a
kind of sly coquetry:)

GIRL: Shall I undress, my Lord?
BECKET: (Who has not moved) Of course.

(The GIRL starts to undress. BECKET looks at her
coldly, absent-mindedly whistling a few bars of his
little march. Suddenly he stops, goes to the GIRL,
stands there dazed and half naked, and seizes her by
the shoulders.)

I hope you're full of noble feelings and that all this
strikes you as pretty shabby?

(A SERVANT runs in wildly and halts in the
doorway speechless. Before he can speak, the KING
comes stumbling in.)

KING: (Soberly) I had no pleasure with her, Thomas. She let
me lay her down in the litter, limp as a corpse, and
then suddenly she pulled out a little knife from some-
where. There was blood everywhere . . . I feel quite
sick. (BECKET has let go of the GIRL. The KING
adds, haggard:) She could easily have killed me instead!
(A pause. He says abruptly:) Send that girl away. I'm

sleeping in your room tonight. I'm frightened. (BECKET motions to the SERVANT, who takes away the half-naked GIRL. The KING has thrown himself, fully dressed, onto the bed with an animal-like sigh.) Take half the bed.

BECKET: I'll sleep on the floor, my prince.

KING: No. Lie down beside me. I don't want to be alone to-night. (He looks at him and murmurs:) You loathe me, I shan't even be able to trust you now . . .

BECKET: You gave me your Seal to keep, my prince. And the Three Lions of England which are engraved on it keep watch over me too.

KING: (His voice already thick with sleep) I shall never know what you're thinking . . .

(BECKET has thrown a fur coverlet over the KING. He lies down beside him and says quietly:)

BECKET: It will be dawn soon, my prince. You must sleep. To-morrow we are crossing to the Continent. In a week we will face the King of France's army and there will be simple answers to everything at last.

(He has lain down beside the KING. A pause, during which the KING's snoring gradually increases. Suddenly, the KING moans and tosses in his sleep.)

KING: (Crying out) They're after me! They're after me! They're armed to the teeth! Stop them! Stop them!

(BECKET sits up on one elbow. He touches the KING, who wakes up with a great animal cry.)

BECKET: My prince . . . my prince . . . sleep in peace. I'm here.

KING: Oh . . . Thomas, it's you . . . They were after me.

(He turns over and goes back to sleep with a deep sigh. Gradually he begins to snore again, softly. BECKET is still on one elbow. Almost tenderly, he draws the coverlet over the KING.)

BECKET: My prince . . . If you were my true prince, if you were one of my race, how simple everything would be. How tenderly I would love you, my prince, in an ordered world. Each of us bound in fealty to the other, head, heart and limbs, with no further questions to ask of oneself, ever. (A pause. The KING'S snores grow louder. BECKET sighs and says with a little smile:) But I cheated my way, a twofold bastard, into the ranks, and found a place among the conquerors. You can sleep peacefully, though, my prince. So long as Becket is obliged to improvise his honor, he will serve you. And if one day, he meets it face to face . . . (A short pause.) But where is Becket's honor?

(He lies down with a sigh, beside the KING. The KING'S snores grow louder still. The candle sputters. The lights grow even dimmer . . .)

THE CURTAIN FALLS

CONCLUSION

The readings in this book represent a miniscule sampling of materials that have accumulated for nine hundred years. They pose some of the questions that historians, novelists, poets, preachers, and playwrights have pondered for generation upon generation, broad questions about the nature of power in society, about the interaction between personal rivals, about forces of change in conflict with forces resisting change.

What about the two principals, Henry and Becket? Was the king a tyrant, ruthless and perfidious, as Milman and others suggest? Or was he, in spite of the acknowledged Angevin temper, a reasonable advocate of legitimate goals, frustrated by the stubbornness of the archbishop and his allies? Was he, as Stubbs suggests, " a moderate and politic conqueror," or did he seek, as Berington writes, "to gratify revenge, and to triumph in the humiliation of a man who had dared to oppose him?"

Did Henry try to take advantage of the good will of his friend, or did Becket reject and attack the friend who had promoted him from the obscurity of his low estate to the second most powerful position in the land? Was Becket an ambitious climber who used and then turned against those who had helped him, including the king?

Perhaps the issue was entirely separate from personalities, and the two comrades whose intimacy turned to bitter hostility were simply victims of pressure neither could withstand. If so, what were the sources of the pressure? Was it the growth of a centralized monarchy, whose full development required control over courts, castles, and income? Was the church a major impediment to its growth? Or conversely, was the burgeoning interest in canon law (whose disciples included Becket as well as Pope Alexander III and John of Salisbury) the new force, while Henry's followers upheld a feudal reaction against it? Pollock and Maitland point out that starting with Henry's time "the lay courts rather than the spiritual are the aggressors and the victors in nearly every contest."

One need not base his judgment on the ultimate direction that legal and political history took. In other words, because national states became stronger, controlling the courts, and the church disappeared from the legal sphere, it does not therefore follow that in the 1160's Henry's party was right and Becket's party was wrong. The question is, what forces were operating most strongly in the twelfth century and for what reasons?

A separate question that this volume raises is: how have the different centuries viewed the controversy? Were twelfth-century writers concerned about the same questions that concerned nineteenth-century writers. If they were different, how and why were they different? Did the nineteenth-century sense of history as progress affect its interpretation of the Becket affair? Have twentieth-century writers lost interest in its issues, or has the interest taken new forms?

In reading twelfth-century exchanges of letters and the accounts of writers like Roger of Hoveden, William of Newburgh, and Edward Grim, how can we distinguish historical truth from emotional self-interest? Later interpretations, including those of the twentieth century, will help our understanding, but essentially the student's job is to evaluate the credibility of witnesses from other ages just as he would evaluate a contemporary columnist's view of current affairs or evidence in a courtroom during a trial.

Finally, this volume departs from traditional practice by introducing fictional accounts of three dramatists. This raises certain additional questions. How legitimate are the conclusions of the playwrights when we compare them with their sources of information? How much of our daily sense of "what is history" comes from films, novels, and legends? How does the serious student of history compensate for conclusions that come from such sources?

The sifting and balancing of these bits of evidence is now the student's task. His composite conclusion may not represent final historical truth in any objective sense, but it should evolve from intelligent analysis of the raw material that makes up historical truth.

BIBLIOGRAPHICAL ESSAY

Students who are investigating this topic for the first time can profitably use one or more of the standard text books on English history as starting points. An old but thoroughly reliable and readable one by William E. Lunt, *History of England* (Harper & Brothers, New York, 1938) is probably the best. More recent and of particular value for its introduction of newer interpretations is Warren C. Hollister, *The Making of England* (D. C. Heath, Boston, 1966), especially Chapter 5. Other standard texts include Walter P. Hall, Robert G. Albion, and Jennie Barnes Pope, *A History of England and the Commonwealth* (Ginn and Co., New York, fourth edition, 1961); and David Harris Willson, *A History of England* (Holt, Rinehart and Winston, New York, 1967).

An excellent English translation of basic source materials is Volume II, *English Historical Documents*, edited by David Douglas and George W. Greenaway (Oxford University Press, New York, 1953). Covering the period 1042 to 1189, it includes a body of Becket materials, especially on pages 702 to 780. The letters from Alexander III to Becket, the selections from Edward Grim's biography, and the writs of Henry II that are used in this book are taken from that volume. Another useful item is George W. Greenaway, editor, William Fitz Stephen, *The Life and Death of Thomas Becket* (Folio Society, London, 1961), which is basically a chronologically arranged collection of data held together by the editor's explanatory comments. *Sources of English Constitutional History*, edited and translated by Carl Stephenson and Frederick G. Marcham (Harper & Brothers, New York, 1937) contains a well-annotated translation of the Constitutions of Clarendon (see above), as well as other documentary materials.

The student hardy enough to explore the original Latin and Norman French should investigate the Rolls Series, most particularly the volumes edited by James C. Robertson and J. B. Sheppard, *Materials for the History of Thomas Becket, Archbishop of Canterbury*, 7 volumes, (Longman and Co., London, 1875–85). The spate of biographies of Becket began almost immediately after his assassination, including those by William of Canterbury, William Fitz Stephen, Herbert of Bosham, and John of Salisbury, all of whom had known the archbishop for years. The one by Edward Grim and those by Benedict of Peterborough and Alan of Tewksbury are also included in that series. An Icelandic writer, Erikr Magnüsson, soon followed with an additional account.

Some twelfth-century chronicles have been translated into English, including those by Roger of Hoveden and William of Newburgh. The work entitled *Gesta Regis Hendici Secundi (Deeds of King Henry II)* is a record representing official court views and is probably the source of information and even wording for the earlier period of Roger's narrative. Robert of Torigny, who became abbot of Mont St. Michel, kept an account of Norman history for much of Henry II's reign, as did Gervase, a monk at Canterbury from 1163 to about 1210. Walter Map's *De Nugis Curialium* (available in a translation called *Courtier's Trifles*), while not directly related to the topic of this book, contains amusing and personal anecdotes from Henry's court.

A basic reference work for students of English history is *The Dictionary of National Biography*, which contains sketches of all the major figures in the controversy. Most articles are followed by brief bibliographical notes indicating leads to various primary sources.

The past centuries have contributed a broad range of secondary materials, ranging in quality from high level of excellence to virtual uselessness. The strong element of presentism in the contemporary university climate of opinion should not lead students to rely on the recentness of publication date as a sole criterion of value. Even those writers who are now under considerable attack, such as Bishop Stubbs, J. R. Green, Horace Round, and some of their contemporaries need to be examined if for no other reason than to comprehend what the attack is all about. But there are other reasons for reading them, and our own generation must not fall into the trap of assuming that its wisdom represents the only fount of historical truth.

For example, the three-volume *History of the Life of King Henry II and of the Age in Which he Lived*, by George Lord Lyttelton (Faulkner, Dublin, 1768), for all its faults and bias, is a more complete biography of Henry than any other. R. W. Eyton, *Court, Household, and Itinerary of King Henry II* (Taylor, London, 1878) is invaluable for details of place and time. There does not exist any biography of the Plantagenet King that can be termed definitive, but John T. Appleby, *Henry II* (Bell, London, 1962) is a good, up-to-date introduction to the reign. Earlier accounts include L. F. Salzmann, *Henry II* (Houghton Mifflin, New York, 1914) and Mrs. J. R. Green, *Henry the Second* (Macmillan, London, 1888), both sketchy and with no pretense to depth. Others include Sir Arthur Helps, *King Henry the Second* (Pickering, London, 1843) and another current volume, Richard W. Barber, *Henry Plantagenet* (Barrie and Rockliff, London, 1964).

Becket has been more fortunate, at least quantitatively, in his biographers. Many from the nineteenth century represent only altered versions of earlier hagiography, although some offer critical insights and strong viewpoints. The list includes Clement W. Barraud, *St. Thomas of Canterbury* (Longmans, London, 1892); the pro-monarchy account by James Anthny Froude, *Life and Times of Thomas Becket* (Scribner, Armstrong and Co., New York 1878); Henry H. Milman, *Life of Thomas Becket* (Sheldon and Co., New York, 1860); John Morris, *Life and Martyrdom of St. Thomas Becket* (Burns and Oates, London, 1885); Lewis B. Radford, *Thomas of London before his Consecration* (University Press, Cambridge, 1894); and James G. Robertson, *Becket, Archbishop of Canterbury* (J. Murray, London, 1859).

Interest has not stopped in the twentieth century, but it is hard to find anything that can clearly be called a reinterpretation. Much of the writing continues with the basic themes and variations already developed. Exceptions to this are the excellent and thoughtful writings of David Knowles, *The Episcopal Colleagues of Thomas Becket* (University Press, Cambridge, 1951), and *Archbishop Thomas Becket, A Character Study* (Cumerlege, London, 1939). Aspects worth exploring are found in Paul A. Brown, *The Development of the Legend of Thomas Becket* (Philadelphia, 1930); also in the fairly traditional volume by

William H. Hutton, *Thomas Becket* (University Press, Cambridge, 1926). The most recent, and probably the best, general account is by Richard Winston, *Thomas Becket* (A. Knopf, New York, 1967) where one finds a full summary of the known material for the popular reader.

For a general and thorough analysis of the whole period, William Stubbs, *Historical Introduction to the Rolls Series* (Longmans, Green, London, 1902) is excellent for its stimulating, provocative essays.

In addition to the three plays from which cuttings were taken for this volume, many other fictionalized versions exist. Among the more recent are two historical novels, Shelley Mydans, *Thomas* (Doubleday, Garden City, 1965) and Alfred Duggan, *My Life for My Sheep* (Dutton, New York, 1955). The many plays include Christopher Fry's *Curtmantle* and an early nineteenth-century production once claimed as a long-lost work of Shakespeare's.

The full list of related references is extensive, and students may usefully find bibliographical assistance from Charles Gross, *The Sources and Literature of English History from the Earliest Times to 1485* (Longmans, Green, London, 1915), for the earlier materials; and journal accounts and reviews, particularly those in the *American Historical Review*, for more recent items. The text book by Lunt, cited above, has a good bibliography, as do the volumes of the *Oxford History of England*.